CRIMSON

A TRUE STORY OF A WOMAN STAINED BY
SEXUAL ABUSE

CLAIRE WREN

Published 2024
Printed in the United States of America
Second Edition

This first edition of this book was previously published by Somebody Loves You Publishing under ISBN 978-1-934820-28-5 and LCCN 2016960687.

ISBN (softcover): 978-1-963380-76-7
ISBN (e-book): 978-1-963380-77-4

For information, address:
Holzer Books LLC
8 The Green, Ste. A
Dover, Delaware 19901 USA

For information about special discounts available for bulk purchases, sales promotions, and educational needs, contact:
info@holzerbooksllc.com
+1 (888) 901-7776

Contents

Dedication

The pages penned into this book are lovingly dedicated to my beloved family. All have suffered in some way from the immense emotional and physical damage of sexual abuse, especially my two dearest sisters and my nieces.

This book is bound with a firm message of hope and healing for the countless other victims and their suffering families.

It is also dedicated to my children, whom I dearly love. They, at times, have had to count the cost with me, as I have served the Lord Jesus Christ.

Special thanks to my Pastor's wife, Sharon Ries, faithful friend and comrade, in whose life path God chose to place me. I am indebted to her discipleship in Christ which has deepened my own walk with God, my Savior. Her words of encouragement led me to write this book.

Finally, this book is dedicated to England, my cherished childhood home, in hopes of a needed revival. In past history, England was known for having a rich, Christian, spiritual heritage; this heritage, rooted in the God of the Bible, has sadly been forgotten.

If My people who are called by My name will humble themselves, and pray and seek My face, and turn from their wicked ways, then I will hear from heaven, and will forgive their sin and heal their land.

2 CHRONICLES 7:14

Preface

Our Father which art in heaven,
Hallowed be thy name.
Thy kingdom come,
Thy will be done in earth,
On earth as it is in heaven . . .

Three little girls, tucked in bed, harmoniously sang
this verse to their own sweet, made-up tune. Three
little sisters sang joyfully to a God they did not know
personally—to a God who nevertheless watched
over them. They sang together the words repeatedly,
until sleepiness took over, and they simultaneously
fell peacefully asleep. Each small girl went through
years of secret sexual abuse. One grew up and God
became known to her . . . He became her Deliverer . . .
that young girl was me . . .

Dealing with the constant memories and emotional
scars of sexual abuse, or any forcible violation, is
extremely difficult. These deeply inflicted wounds do
not easily heal. If left alone to fester, these neglected
injuries of sexual abuse will remain unhealed. Many
violated women then suffer a continual, secret pain.
When something triggers a terrifying memory from
their past, their anguish will resurface. But there is
hope in a God of love who cares and is acquainted
with the sufferings of the innocent . . . It is God
alone who can heal these open wounds. Through the
miracle of forgiveness, He works to bring closure to a
woman's dark past and helps her open the door into
a bright, new future.

Introduction

CRIMSON CRIMES

Crimson . . . the deepest rich red, velvet color that can represent, among many other things, the deepest stains of lustful passions unleashed against a woman. Rape, molestation and sexual abuse of any kind bring to mind a woman's worst nightmare. These awful words bring to surface the spine-chilling reality of crimson crimes committed, largely by men, against women of all ages.

If a room full of women began to talk about sexual abuse, you would discover that a large majority, in one way or another, has been sexually violated. Disturbingly, their conversations would reveal the perpetrators to be someone close within the family—a father, uncle or even a grandfather. Other instances of sexual abuse uncover a trusted teacher, priest, neighbor or a babysitter. Even if you are not a victim yourself, you stand a good chance of knowing someone who has been sexually violated.

Being violated may be a past perversion against you as an innocent child, a naïve adolescent, or a mature adult. Acts of violation include: having a tongue forced down one's throat, indecent exposure, molestation, incest and rape, whether or not it is statutory, acquaintance, date or gang rape. An ongoing problem, even in today's society, is sex trafficking, where girls are taken, abducted and sold, to be used for illicit prostitution.

Whatever the crimes committed against you were, there are people, even from your family, who firmly believe that your sexual abuse should remain private—nobody should ever know. After all, they consider it to be nobody else's business, and besides, it is better for everyone that way. What happened behind closed doors should remain behind closed doors. Whatever was spoken and committed in secret should remain unspoken—the secret should be kept silent.

Like dirt swept and hidden under a thick carpet, your sexual abuse remains a hidden secret; nothing is ever disclosed, perhaps for the rest of your life. Nothing seen, nothing heard, or should it be? I have chosen to open wide the door to my life, to tell the world my own story of being sexually violated. My life, after all, is an open book . . .

Chapter One

SEASONS OF INNOCENCE

England . . . a land of rolling hills, village cottages, covered with quaint thatched roofs and neatly kept flowered gardens . . . such a beautiful countryside. The wide open fields are divided by rows of thick bushes, with occasional gates, hemming in the many free-roaming farm animals.

Patch-colored cows slowly chew the cud, while their large, brown eyes stare emptily into the distance, whereas, other cows melodiously moo lowly, slowly treading their hoofs from one side to the other, turning the soggy soil beneath them into glorious mud. White, woolly sheep look like cotton wool[1] dotting the deep green landscape.

Yet, another splendid sight to see, spirited horses—barebacked, tails high and galloping freely. England is a well-watered garden, kept vibrant green by heavy bouts of rain, which is why you always need a brolly.[2]

---

[1] cotton wool: a cotton ball or a wad of cotton.
[2] brolly: an umbrella.

I, Claire Ellen Webster, was born in England's green and pleasant land on August 29, 1959, in Park Royal at the Central Middlesex Hospital. My mother, Jennifer Elizabeth Webster, formerly Wren, and father, Gilbert Lesley Webster, were both happy to have their first little girl. My middle name, Ellen, was the name of a favored aunt on my mother's side of the family. We lived in the outskirts of London, the sub-district in the county of Middlesex. In a society where class is well defined, we were a working class family. Even though I was born in a sub-district sounding like I was royalty, I was as common as they come.

Safe At Home

Everyone wants to reflect back on happy memories of their childhood. I am no different and have recaptured fond memories during the different seasons of the year.

In 1963, our growing family moved from our home in Ealing, where the faint memories of a small, cold and dark home turned into clearer memories of a new home in Northolt, Middlesex. It must have been winter, as it was still dark early and freezing cold.

I was just four years old, and yet, I can still clearly remember peering out of the French glass window door into the gloomy darkness to vaguely see the back garden. At the time, it was just a mound of over-turned dirt with not one flower!

The living room had big, beautiful bay windows that would let in streams of light during a sunny day. How I loved the sunlight and the long summer days, but for now it was dismally dark. Our new home was much bigger. It had three bedrooms, one bathroom upstairs and one small bathroom downstairs. Of course, in England, we commoners would simply refer to it as the *loo*. There was a small closet under the stairs—ah the stairs—a banister to slide down!

Mother and father had more children, six altogether, and our names all began with the letter C. There were three boys and three girls. I remember very clearly the day when our youngest brother was brought home from the hospital. We all eagerly awaited his arrival at the front door; he entered our happy home wrapped tightly in a blanket. Poor dear, being the baby of the family he was always being dressed up in dolls' clothing and placed in our toy prams.[3] He had three older sisters to deal with.

We also had a half-brother, Christopher Wren. He was my mother's firstborn; he had a different father, and he lived with my nana and grandfather in Welwyn Garden City,[4] Hertfordshire. It was a hushed up, scarlet scandal, and none of us ever knew why. In those days you did not ask questions, and people did not talk openly about their private lives.

---

[3] prams: a vehicle for moving a baby around that consists of a small bed supported by a frame on four wheels.

[4] Welwyn Garden City: "a garden town" in England.

In *Jolly old England,* children started school at a very early age. Most nursery age children began at three, but at the tender age of four, I attended Down Manor Infant School. My first teacher was Mrs. Vanstone, and she described me as a very quiet and shy little girl. Her inviting classroom was glistening with hand-made Christmas decorations that the children had made for the merry season. In one corner was an area where you could dress up in play clothes, and I would put on what I thought were the most beautiful, flowing dresses and play pretend . . . just pretend.

Summer

From the moment we arrived to our new home, father began, year after year, to slowly transform our home and garden into a place of beauty. An Englishman's pride is his garden, and his home is his castle. The mounded dirt on one side of the house was turned into a beautiful rose garden. Our garden was the perfect place to relax on the sunny summer weekends. It became a sweet haven to me, especially the rose garden, where the roses grew and blossomed. I could always be found there among the pleasant fragrances.

I spent hours nurturing the roses, sometimes in playful solitude with my own thoughts. At other times, with my two younger sisters, we would pick beautiful pink rose petals and crush them to make perfume. Our mixture of water and rose petals turned into a very muddy brown color that never smelled very pretty, but we had fun playing.

Every summer morning we would wake up to the chirping songs of birds—little sparrows, finches and robins—singing and flitting from the green trees and bushes. As English children, our garden was like our own private sanctuary. We were in a made-up world of our own, playing among the wildflowers . . . buttercups and daisies . . . twirling in a circle as we sung the old nursery rhyme:

"Ring around the rosie . . . a pocket full of posies,
A-tissue! A-tissue! We all fall down!"

Every year my father would do something new to our garden. He laid a paved garden path, then built a rockery[5] and later constructed a glass greenhouse where tomatoes and other plants grew. I watched, fascinated, as he planted tiny seeds. The seeds grew into young seedlings, and when the time was right, father would transfer them into the rich, soft soil of our growing garden.

Often he would give us a shovel, and when horses passed by, he would send us to collect the horse manure—a fresh treasure to place on the soil; I supposed this was good for the plants. He also had a huge compost heap; anything dead from the garden was placed there to decompose and then placed back around the growing plants. My father indeed

---

[5] rockery: an area within a garden that has plants growing between piles of stones.

was gifted with a green thumb, for he could grow anything!

On the weekends, the entire family would enjoy the garden. As innocent little girls, we three sisters would run around in our knickers.[6] I loved to run and feel the gentle, warm breeze on my face and the tousling of my loose curly hair across my bare shoulders.

The garden was a place to enjoy outdoor picnics and play all manner of games: statues,[7] hopscotch, badminton and the well-known game of English cricket. We also rode small bikes or scooters. We girls enjoyed pretending to be mothers with dolls pushed in prams and pushchairs.[8]

Some days it even got warm enough for us to enjoy a small paddling pool. In the mid-afternoon, all six children eagerly listened for the familiar, pleasant tunes of the neighborhood ice cream van that came around every day at the same time. Ice cream was not always affordable, so we considered it a special, delicious treat.

Imagine, six licking tongues not quite quick enough to stop the ice cream from melting under the hot sun, dripping down onto our sun-tanned, bare chests.

---

[6] knickers: women's or girl's underpants.
[7] statues: a game of freeze tag.
[8] pushchairs: a stroller.

On one side of our home in Northolt spanned huge, open, country fields. Even further was a thick wooded area, and beyond the woods was a private farm with free roaming cows. As a family, we would go on very long walks together. The fields and woods were full of discoveries; small ponds were full of newts and tadpoles to catch and place in glass jars.

There was an old, deserted firing range with some broken, brick walls and a rusty, dented, long pole where men came and shot their guns. Father was the only one strong enough to swing across that pole.

Deep in the woods, he bravely climbed all kinds of trees—right up to the very top, where he would disappear out of our sight. Following in our father's footsteps, we learned to climb and hang upside down on England's old, rugged trees. Within the woods grew wild blackberry bushes—ah, juicy berries there for the taking! As we picked away, often getting scratched by the brambles, we ate some, and the rest we delightfully carried home. Warm blackberry crumble with creamy custard was always a favorite treat.

We lived in a relatively safe neighborhood, and we were free to walk to the local shops, our friends' houses or to the local park on our own. Most of our summer days were spent at the park, and home was close enough so we could run home for dinner, quickly eat and go racing back out again. The swings were my favorite; I loved swinging and would often leap off in mid-air as if flying.

One day while swinging, I looked straight before me and saw a large, rugged, brown cross that hung the entire length of one side of the local Baptist Church. The church was more modern than some of the ancient church buildings in England, with their beautiful stained-glass windows. Churches were on every corner; most were either Protestant or Catholic. I can still remember how pleasant it was to hear the melodious sounds of the Catholic Church bells that rang every Sunday morning.

In England, most children are christened—sprinkled with holy water as babies. It is an old tradition, erroneously teaching that you must be christened to become a part of the family of God and, upon death, have the assurance that you will go to heaven. This act of baby baptism constituted a Christian faith, and if asked, "When did you become a Christian?" you would proudly answer that you were a Christian since birth.

Church was left to all of us as an option, so I decided to attend the Girl Guides[9]—a type of Girl Scouts—held close to my home in the Baptist Church building. There I was taught to recite:

"I promise that I will do my best, to love my God,
To serve the Queen and my country,
To help other people and to keep the Guide law."

---

[9] Girl Guides: a sister organization of the Girl Scouts and was founded in Britain in 1910.

My young life was not only filled with some religious traditions, but also a lot of superstition. Mother carried a rabbit's foot with her for good luck. She taught us a velvet black cat walking in front of you was a sign of good luck, and walking under a ladder, bad luck. Never leave new shoes on a table or put an umbrella up in the house, as this was also bad luck, and red and white flowers together meant death. I clearly remember my mother's frightened face, along with her fearful correction, when I forgot and did any of those things. She also loved traveling gypsies and would give them food or money to have her palm read. She told us that to slight them might bring a curse!

During the warm summer nights, daylight lasted longer, almost until ten o'clock, but bedtime came early, and it was very difficult to go straight to sleep. So, my sisters and I would play, talk and sing songs together—one favorite was *Our Father which Art in Heaven,* which we sang to our own made-up tune. However, if we made too much noise and did not go to sleep when we should, we would have a visit from our angry father. We soon learned to fear our father. He would take off his belt and give us all a good hiding.[10] We would scream as loud as we could, in hopes to gain some kind of mercy, but mercy never came.

---

[10] hiding: in British slang, a 'hiding' may refer to a solid beating.

Autumn

Each year as summer ended, autumn brought a new, fresh smell to the crisp, cool air. Breathing in, you could literally sense autumn's arrival; it had a distinct smell that came at the change of the season. As temperatures dropped, when I exhaled my usual warm, invisible breath turned misty white, and I, along with most children, pretended to smoke a cigarette. Most adults smoked cigarettes, and some children, even though illegal, began smoking as early as eleven. So this copycat behavior was never reprimanded.

The tree leaves turned wonderful shades of rich red and orange. Piles of crisp leaves gathered alongside the old, grey curbs. All English children enjoyed jumping in the piles of dead, yet colorful leaves. They dragged their feet through them, sending them flying in every direction, but safely jumping back from the curbside to the pavement whenever a car came whizzing by. Then the children would go running and stomping to crunch the bone dry leaves that landed on the cracked pavements.

Walking turned into a game where they began jumping from pavement to pavement while missing the cracks, singing . . .

"Don't step on the crack or you'll fall
And break your back!"

While wearing our Wellington boots,[11] puddles were splashed in, brollies were always carried, and you could say our seemingly happy childhood left us *Singing in the Rain.*

At this time of year, crane flies—large, winged insects, commonly known as daddy-longlegs—flew about, much to the delight of little schoolboys, who would catch the long-legged creatures within their hands. Then they found a few unsuspecting schoolgirls and gleefully released the creepy looking critters right underneath their moderate uniform skirts. Quite amused with themselves, the schoolboys crowded together, laughing hysterically, as the girls went screaming down the street; this they did in all good, harmless fun.

It was never pleasant to arise from one's cozy, warm bed to brace the chilly, often foggy, walk to school. School days began to drag, and walking home was not much fun either. The dreary skies darkened by late afternoons, and children returned home in the dark.

Anticipation broke the monotony of school as soon it would be the fifth of November, Fireworks Day. Guy Fawkes, a traitor in 17th Century English history, was captured while plotting to blow up the Houses of Parliament, in hopes of killing King James I

---

[11] Wellington boots: a water proof boot that reaches almost to the knee, also known as rubber boots or wellies. They were worn and popularized by Arthur Wellesley 1st Duke of Wellington.

of England, on 5 November, 1605. He was tried, *hung, drawn and quartered*[12]—a torturous, horrid and cruel death. English schools taught their young pupils a commemorative poem and the famous, gruesome history of it all.

Remember, Remember the Fifth of November

Remember, remember the fifth of November
Gunpowder, treason and plot.
I see no reason why gunpowder, treason
Should ever be forgot . . .

Guy Fawkes, 'twas intent
To blow up the king and parliament
Three score barrels of powder below
Poor old England to overthrow.

By God's providence he was catched
With a dark lantern and burning match.
Holloa[13] boys Holloa boys
God save the King!
Hip hip Hooray!
Hip hip Hooray!

(Author Unknown)

---

[12] *hung, drawn and quartered:* this grisly phrase is the proper name for the death sentence beginning in 13th century England. It was a punishment for traitors; men who committed treason.

[13] Holloa: a cry for attention or encouragement, a very loud utterance.

Excited children stood outside any sweet shops with a propped up *Guy* made from father's old clothing stuffed with used newspapers. They loudly chanted, "Penny for the *Guy!*" in hopes of getting money for their fireworks.

On the cold eve of November 5, our excited family gathered in our garden—darkened by night. Soon a blazing bonfire gave us welcomed heat, as it consumed in its flames the makeshift[14] *Guy* that we had placed on top of old, broken furniture, along with anything else we found to be burned. Staring wide-eyed at the sky, we would watch the many exploding fireworks. Then with our hands protected and tucked snuggly in knitted gloves, our parents lit and gave to each of us the most loved handheld fireworks—the sparklers! Much to everyone's delight, they burst into spitting sparks of light as we twirled them around in circles.

Winter

Winter arrived, forming long, glistening, cone-shaped icicles that hung from our home's window ledges. Reaching out of the window, we could snap off the icicles and lick them like giant lollipops. Our mother would bundle us up as warm as she could, so that we could play outside in the powder fresh snow that lay on the freezing ground.

---

[14] makeshift: done or made using whatever is available.

We gathered together plenty of snow to make our first snowman. We used a large carrot for his nose and black lumps of coal for his eyes. Once satisfied with Mr. Snowman, we would begin throwing snowballs in every direction, as we all ran as best we could for safe cover.

Before we turned blue from the cold, we eagerly ran back into our home's warm front room, where a cozy fire was burning. Our gloves were sopping wet and in need of drying—off they came as we held up our little hands close to the flames, warming ourselves, while mother brought us welcomed, hot cups of tea or cocoa.

An outside coal bunker was used to store coal, our winter fuel. When I grew tall enough, I would fill up the coal bucket and bring it inside. Father would light a fire under the coal using old newspapers and matches. I used to love cleaning the fireplace and sweeping out the dusty, old ashes. The cold, black coals glowed a warm red color when heated, as if inviting everyone in the house to come closer.

Poor families usually heated only one room; everywhere else in the house was left freezing cold. Richer people did not need to huddle over an open fire. They could afford expensive central heating that conveniently heated the whole house.

Even taking a bath or doing laundry was very costly. Bath time was generally once a week on a Sunday. Usually my sisters and I took a bath in the same bath water; then the boys took a bath after us. Sometimes it was the other way around, but we were always worried they had peed in the water! If we splashed around too much, we got in trouble, because once we had caused flooding when water dripped through the ceiling.

The cold weather limited us from outdoor play, so we often just stayed indoors in the one heated room. Thick coloring books, board games and puzzles kept our young minds busy. *Hide-and-Go-Seek* and *I Spy with My Little Eye* were among our favorite house games. A small library van would visit the neighborhood, and checked out books were devoured.

Our beds in winter were layered with thick blankets, and the flannel sheets were not only cold but damp. Once we were tucked in bed, the warmth from our small bodies, combined with a hot water bottle placed at our feet, kept us well insulated; then sleep would finally take over.

During the week, a quick wash every morning from a sink filled with hot water was all that we needed before we went off to school. Mum would make sure we had our clean school uniforms, socks and underwear ready the night before. We walked to school like everyone did, no matter what the weather.

After infant school[15] was completed, primary school[16] began, where instruction was given to proper posture. Whether sitting behind a desk or standing, it was told to us, "Chest out, stomach in, shoulders back and legs straight!"

Mr. Edwards, the school's Headmaster,[17] would walk between the ranks of very nervous children. He held a long, curved cane that nobody wanted to feel across their bottoms—needless to say he was very well respected. The only time that cane came close to me was to tap at the bottom of my hymn book as I was singing. The book needed to be raised slightly higher in proper position.

During school assemblies, we sang hymns and said prayers. As Christmas time drew near, carols were sung instead, and the famous Charles Dickens story, *A Christmas Carol,* was performed. I played a part behind the scenes of *Marley the Ghost* and got to rattle his heavy, long chains. I sternly warned Scrooge, in a scary ghostlike voice, of death and judgment to come, if he would not take the opportunity to change.

Then the story every child was taught in English schools at Christmas time was reenacted, the Nativity—Mary, Joseph and baby Jesus. Only one girl would have the honor of being chosen to be Mary in this important play. It became a serene time of

---

[15] infant school: a school or part of a school for children who are four to seven.

[16] primary school: a school for children from the age's seven to eleven, or an elementary school.

[17] Headmaster: principal.

reflection for the well-dressed parents attending the production, as they proudly, and often tearfully, watched their young, innocent children trying to remember their lines and proclaiming the angels' message of, "Glory to God in the highest and on earth peace, goodwill towards men!"

In this wintery season, the colorful holly bushes[18] grew. Their bright crimson berries fell, often crushed under the feet of passers-by, splashing red against the white snow. According to legend, we learned that the holly bush was named *The Holy Bush*, as their sharp thorns represented the piercing thorns of Christ's crown. The crimson berries pictured the warm drops of blood that dripped from the Son of God's forehead. Like the berries, He too was crushed by sinners who crucified Him on the cross. Traditionally, the luscious, winter green leaves of the holly bush, with their crimson colored berries, were used to decorate English homes at Christmas time—a reminder of the Gospel[19] message not fully understood by me.

As we anticipated Christmas Day, my sisters and I would joyfully sing Christmas carols together at bedtime—*Rudolph the Red Nose Reindeer, The Holly and the Ivy, Once in Royal David's City* and *Away in a Manger*—until we were tired and sleep once again took over.

---

[18] holly bushes: the holly, or prickly bush, is a shrub of the evergreen species.
[19] Gospel: the Good News of Jesus' birth, life, death and resurrection, recorded in Matthew, Mark, Luke and John.

Mother was quite the homemaker and was always singing while cleaning. She reminded me of Snow White, who always happily sang whilst[20] she *tidied up the place* of the seven dwarfs' dusty and dirty home. Winter to me was a cozy time; mother would knit us jumpers, cardigans, warm scarves and hats. She made us girls the prettiest, silky, pink curtains for our bedroom, as she sat in her comfortable chair sewing in front of the electric floor heater that glowed warmly.

In fact, as the oldest daughter, I was well taught the art of homemaking, having the responsibilities of washing, ironing, cleaning and cooking. Laundry was piled high and then thrown down the stairs. We tumbled down with the laundry, landing safely in a heap at the bottom. Wet laundry, hung on the long washing line, was stiffened and dried by winter winds, then ironed to become soft and unwrinkled. Even our underwear was ironed!

However, the frigid, cold winter had a dreadful downside for me, for that is when I, along with my siblings, was mostly sick. In the summer we were well and could escape outside.

One year my middle sister, who was the sickliest, nearly died from pneumonia. Hospital tests were done on all six of us; four of us were diagnosed with Cystic Fibrosis—a killer disease of the pancreas that

---

[20] whilst: during the time when something happens.

caused the lungs to be filled with thick mucus. A doctor sadly pronounced our death sentences. A child with Cystic Fibrosis usually died from suffocation by the age of sixteen.

We never knew how deathly sick we were; it was kept from us. We went to the hospital for yearly check-ups, including chest X-rays and blood work. On those special hospital visits, mother would always dress us girls up in identical new outfits; we arrived looking nice and well taken care of.

Mother had to work, sometimes taking on jobs within the home, making Christmas crackers.[21] At other times, she worked away from home—often waitressing. In these times, we missed her, as each of us deeply loved our mother and often fought for her love, attention and approval. When Mother was gone, Father stayed home during the day, often sleeping due to the night shift he had worked.

Spring

As the snow slowly melted, patches of vibrant green grass appeared, and small, chirping birds visited the exposed areas, looking for worms and tiny insects. The fragrant flowers sprang up, butterflies fluttered and danced on the fresh spring breeze, and my world became a myriad of rainbow colors that

---

[21] Christmas crackers: a tube of brightly colored paper, usually given at Christmas parties or dinners that make a noise when pulled apart. They usually contain small presents and a paper crown.

blazed the new scenery. With spring melting away the dismal darkness of winter, people were happier, depressive moods left, and frowned, cold faces now softened to smiles and rosy cheeks. Children were eager to be outside once more; their voices of play and pranks filled the warmer spring air.

Once the earth was dried, children climbed the rolling hills which were clothed with soft, new grass, and tumbled down, right to the very bottom. Dizzy children stood, caught their balance, and bolted back up to the top of the hill slopes only to tumble back down again and again.

For some reason, spring was the season I remember losing my baby teeth! When I, or any of my siblings, had a loose, wiggly tooth, it was pulled out the old-fashioned way. A long, cotton string was tied around the tooth. The other part was tied to an open door handle. The door was quickly slammed shut, and, for the most part, it worked. The yanked, small, bloody tooth was then placed under the pillow for a shilling[22] left by the tooth fairy—Father or Mother.

On happy days, our home was filled with classical or modern music that played on an old record player. As usual, Mother sang along while doing her housework. These old LP's and 45 single, vinyl records needed to be handled carefully, so as not to scratch them or break the fragile phonographic needle.

---

[22] shilling: a unit of money used in Britain until 1971.

Every Sunday afternoon was family time, and together we gathered around our new colored television. Broadway musicals and the best, old, western movies simply mesmerized us.

With spring, came Easter and a nice two-week break from school. Boiled eggs for breakfast came with drawn faces and handcrafted, paper crowns that our father had made. Sliced, buttered toast, called *soldiers,*[23] were dipped in the soft, yellow egg yolk. Large, chocolate eggs were handed out to six very excited children; the chocolate lasted at least a week. Spring brought with it an anticipation of lazy summer days with no school or horrid homework.

These four blended seasons relate the cherished and happy years of my innocent childhood—an ever changing canvas, a portrait of pictures that showed life as it was in the Webster family. I had dedicated parents who worked hard, as they struggled financially to feed such a large family and care for constantly sick children. Six precious, little English children bonded strongly together, playing and growing through all the different seasons of life. To everyone around us—family, neighbors and friends— we were seemingly a big, happy family.

But behind these happy seasons of childhood lay a hidden and sinister secret . . . we were far from normal . . .

---

[23] *soldiers*: thin strips of bread or toast sliced so that they can be dipped into a soft boiled egg with the top of the shell removed.

Chapter Two

STOLEN INNOCENCE

The Abuser

Father was not a handsome man. He was rather short and plain looking, with a partly gold-filled tooth right in the front. He had straight, dark brown, greasy hair, cut razor short in the back and sides. His hair hung longer in the front, combed to one side or straight back, which made him, I thought, look somewhat like Dracula. He suffered badly from arthritis, and, as a young man, he had an ever-so-slight hunch to his shoulders. Dad, as we called him, had natural blue eyes. When he tanned dark in the summer, his eyes popped an even more vibrant blue; at least that helped him look a little more attractive.

As a dedicated father, he worked extremely hard to provide for our large family at an American company named Hoovers,[24] located in Greenford, Middlesex. Hard work was a value he strove to pass on to his children. His fatherly advice to all of us was, "Always make sure you pay your bills." The top priority was to pay the bills first—that kept a roof over your head.

---

[24] Hoovers: originally founded in Ohio, USA in 1908, Hoover Limited became a registered company in the UK in 1919. The first factory, in Perivale in Middlesex, opened in 1932.

Father had been a sergeant in Her Majesty's Army;[25] he had a disciplined lifestyle. He was never late to work. As a regimented man, he rose early, often making us breakfast and helping his children get ready for school. His clothes and shoes were always prepared for the next day, shirts steam-pressed with starched collars and cuffs. Just as if still in the army, he would *spit polish* his black work shoes until he could see his face in the shine. He showed us all how to polish and take care of our shoes. We learned that polishing shoes was a must—first, because shoes were expensive, and second, to protect them against the harsh, English, wet weather.

Seeing as we were not a wealthy family, father, at this time, did not have a car. Trains and buses were not always reliable in bad weather, so his trusted and preferred transportation was a bicycle. Through all kinds of weather, no matter rain, snow, sleet or London fog, there he was, covered in a bright yellow rain poncho, on his sturdy bicycle. Before he went, he placed old-fashioned, metal bicycle clips around his ankles, so that his trousers did not get caught in the spokes of the bicycle wheels. Once ready, off he rode.

Often he worked the grueling night shift and slept during the day. We, six energetic children, had to try hard to keep quiet during the day, or we would face our angry father. So, believe me, we stayed

---

[25] Her Majesty's Army: the British Army; which members swear (or affirm) allegiance to the monarch as commander-in-chief.

pretty quiet. Typically, we all kept to the well-known English phrase, "Children should be seen but not heard." Mother, being wise, would send us to play in the back garden, as their bedroom was upstairs towards the front of the house.

When father was not sleeping or working, he continued to improve our home. He was quite the handyman, good with woodwork and excellent at any kind of decorating. Accidents do happen when handling tools, and on one particular day, while cutting a piece of wood with an electric saw, he cut clean through to the bone of his thumb. He had not felt a thing at first, but when he did, the pain was so excruciating, I remember him running and screaming into the kitchen to frantically wrap the hanging thumb together before heading to the hospital for stitches.

As children, one of the best activities was to help our dad take off the old wallpaper. Together we would wet down the walls and wait for the paper to absorb the water, because when it was wet, it was far easier to remove. Then we got busy scratching away with the scraping tools to peel away the wet wallpaper. It was quite enjoyable really; we could make an absolute mess of the room, trouble free.

Our tidy, humble home was an open door to our many school and neighborhood friends. When they came to play or have dinner, our dad enjoyed making them laugh. He had a very *daft*[26] sense of humor—his jokes were really embarrassing.

Both in our neighborhood and at his workplace, he was known as a very caring and devoted father. Truthfully, he did, to an extent, have admirable qualities. However, despite the outward appearance of a loving, hardworking family man, inwardly he was a man of cloaked deception . . .

Occasionally, Father would drop information concerning other children that seemed to be a part of his life. Like patching pieces of material together that would become a quilt, I had come to find that my mother had been the second woman in his life. He had other children. Father divulged he had a son who died at seven years old. He also had a daughter. Somewhere, I had a half-brother and a half-sister! That is all I ever found out—we lived as if they never existed. He was a fornicator. He had fathered two families. This was unheard of in the days when I grew up.

Later, I would come to understand I was his bastard child born out of wedlock. If neighbors had caught wind of my parents' shameful, lifestyle, they would have delightfully feasted on the revealed scandal—like tasty morsels of *Turkish delight*.[27] His darkest of

---

[26] *daft:* silly or stupid.
[27] *Turkish delight:* gelatinous sweet confectionary made of syrup and corn flour, dusted with icing.

secrets were to become my worst nightmare. Hidden behind his very good reputation, behind closed doors, he practiced perversion. He was hooked on pornography; the magazines, found years later by my brothers, were hidden under the mattress of my parents' double bed. His inflamed and untamed lust caused him to commit unthinkable acts against me—his own, innocent daughter. They were indeed, heinous, crimes.

Molested

I was very young . . . and innocent—perhaps only about six or seven—when I first recalled my father's perversion and acts of molestation. I was in the front room of our home, the central place where the family gathered to watch television, in the room where the sun shone warm streams of light through the large bay windows.

On this day, the windows were shrouded in darkness, the curtains were drawn, and the doors were closed. It was in the darkness that my father sexually abused me, with just the glow of our homely[28] fireplace. I do not remember being undressed, but I do remember the molestation that took place. I stood silent and submissive to Father's authority; I did nothing to resist, but accepted and yielded to whatever he was doing and saying.

---

[28] homely: British language speaks of a place or surroundings that are simple but cozy and comfortable, as one's own home.

At times, my small hands were taught how to satisfy my father's lust, or he would hold my legs tightly together and relieve himself. The sexual abuse continued, and as I grew, so grew my understanding and fear . . .

Fear became the main factor in my unhealthy relationship with my father, who continuously insisted his perverted actions remain completely secret. He sealed the fear by feeding me with what would happen if I was ever to tell. It was as if he had placed a gag across my mouth and tied it himself. His words are forever etched in my memory, along with the fear that kept me scared silent . . .

Being a master manipulator and in complete control of his young daughter, he said,

"Daddy's face will be in the newspapers."

"The police will come to our home and Daddy will be taken to jail."

"Mummy and Daddy will divorce."

"You would not want that to happen would you?"

"All your brothers and sisters will be sent into foster homes, and you will be separated."

"You will be taken away, and you will never see them again."

Then the clincher, the lock and key,

"If you tell, nobody will believe you!"

Words are very powerful. Those few sentences sealed my fate to remain his constant victim. His evil words and threats of what would happen if I told were like chains being bound about my tiny wrist and feet. I understood him completely. There would be no one to help. I could not tell my mother; I could not tell anyone because they would never believe me. While he continued to play the part of a good, wholesome, hardworking father, I was trapped as his prisoner—a victim with no door of escape.

The greater terror than the sexual abuse itself was, as a child, to think about being taken away to live with a complete stranger—taken somewhere and with someone I did not know. My constant mental nightmare was the fear of breaking the strong family bonds between my mother, my brothers and my two dear, little sisters. If it happened, it would be entirely my fault—I would shoulder the guilt.

Father's frightening words became like a heavy millstone around my neck that sank me deep into the muddy mire. A huge weight of responsibility had now been placed on my young shoulders. Keeping my family together was my duty. Such an unfair weight for a little child, but nevertheless, the baggage was mine; I was forced to carry it.

My father's constant, verbal torment worked emotionally and mentally to help brainwash his own little girl into submission and to accept his depraved actions. The only thing left to do was to survive. Interwoven in childhood play with dolls, was my father who played sex. All I was able to do was endure the suffering in silence, like the silence of the lambs before they go to slaughter. The span of the suffering would be years, lasting right into my adolescence.

Silence sealed me to become his victim whenever the opportunities came—sometimes in the dead darkness of night, when I was awakened and quietly led in my nightgown, still half-asleep, into another room to be sexually abused. More frequently, the abuse came during the day. Being a sickly child, I was frequently home alone, at his mercy, without the presence or protection of my mother. It did not matter that I was home sick with fever, the abuse came often. During the sexual abuse, there was a certain numbness—an emotional shutdown that would happen. I could deal with his sexual demands when my emotions were detached. I acted mechanically just to get the abuse over with as quickly as possible.

Father gave me a secret sign when he wanted sexual favors. He would take my small hand and simply rub his finger across my palm. As he stroked my palm, he looked lustfully into my eyes. I knew the hunter was on the hunt; it would only be a matter of time before he had his little deer.

When I became slightly older, money came into play. Sexual favors were rewarded with cash. The most I remember receiving was about half a pound,[29] which is fifty-pence.[30] Unknown to me then, I was like a paid, child prostitute. I earned money to satisfy my father's lust, and, being very young, I would happily run to buy candy with my new earnings.

The years slowly began to pass. Heading into my preteens, I gained some wisdom and learned how to avoid my father like the plague. I spent much more time hanging around my schoolmates who I had grown close to, and, for the most part, I stayed outside with them even in the rain. Trees, bushes, parks and my friends' homes all became safe sanctuaries from my father's abuse. Less time at home meant less sexual abuse. Perhaps, finally, I would have complete relief and be able to move forward and bury my past.

Unbeknownst to me, my two younger sisters, even more vulnerable than myself, had also fallen victim to my father. No doubt he used the same horrid tactics to manipulate them into surrendering. My middle sister, who had the weakest health and spent more time at home, found secret hiding places to conceal her whereabouts from my father. She would lie hidden away under a small, dark, stairway closet or the large bedroom wardrobe, where she felt safe. Eerily, Father would call out her name trying

---

[29] half a pound: is equal to fifty pence or fifty pee, about eighty one cents.
[30] pence: pound and pence is the official currency of the United Kingdom.

to find his victim. She would wait hours on end until she heard her mother's voice—the signal to come out of hiding. Mother was home and home seemed safe. My youngest sister, to this day, will not speak about what happened—she remains tight-lipped, unable to voice to anyone her pain.

Lost

Significant to my troubled young life, and something that would make such an intense impression happened at the age of about twelve. I was attending Walford Secondary Modern School[31] and had joined the cross-country team. I absolutely loved to run. It gave me such a sense of freedom, and by competing in cross-country, I could run at great lengths.

The long cross-country races were always in the chilly winter season, some early on Saturday mornings. On one particular morning, our school team was driven by bus to Horsenden Hill to race against several other schools. Although a wintery cold, dry day, the ground still had clumps of icy snow and was damp from the early morning dew. Horsenden Hill had wide open country fields and a denser, thick, wooded area. The winding race course was marked with bright colored flags along the way. Soon the race was to begin, so everyone stretched,

---

[31] Walford Secondary Modern School: High School ages eleven to sixteen or extended to eighteen.

warmed up and took off their warm, fleece sweats, and in our shorts and school T-shirts, we made for the starting line.

Once off and running, one of my black plimsolls[32] came loose, and I had to keep stopping to slip the shoe back on again. I tried to tighten the laces, so the shoe would stay on. They were probably a little too big, as mother always bought shoes bigger, so they would last longer. Unfortunately, by this time, most of the girls were far ahead of me. Disheartened and frustrated, I lagged behind. Once I lost sight of all the school teams running in front of me, I gave up; miserable, I stopped the race and began to walk aimlessly. For some reason, I no longer saw any flags that marked the way I should go . . . as I wandered, in only a pair of shorts and a T-shirt, I became acutely aware of the biting cold.

Feeling sure that somehow I would find my way back, I kept walking, but everything looked the same. Snow began to fall and lay a thin blanket of white powder upon the frozen ground. Realization of my plight set in. I was lost . . . my stomach sank . . . and fear, my well-known friend, returned as my only companion. You see, in the local newspapers, I had read stories of women who were raped or found murdered on this particular hill. I understood murder, of course, but rape—even though I knew

---

[32] plimsoll: a flat, light shoe made of heavy cloth with rubber sole, worn especially for sports.

it harmed a woman, I still was unsure of its full meaning. My heart raced, anxiety caused pressure in my chest, and my throat dried.

I was terrified, unprotected and vulnerable to anything that might happen. Every sound made me jump nervously. All the weird, creepy noises in the woods easily startled me. Still I wandered . . . numbness set in . . . I became disoriented and utterly bewildered. Tears welled up in my eyes, blurring my vision and running down my cold, red cheeks. As the icy winter day darkened, so did my hopes of being found. Exhausted, weary and oblivious to my surroundings, I eventually stumbled out into a clear wide open field.

Unable to focus completely, in the far distance I saw something deep red. As the object got closer, I recognized the person's face and realized that it was my P.E. teacher, Mrs. Hardcastle, holding a red cape. She raced towards me and hurriedly wrapped it around my shoulders. Genuine worry and concern was written all over her face. A crowd of other adults soon gathered around me, all relieved that I had been found. Apparently, I had meandered in the freezing cold weather for two whole hours, lost in the dense woods, frightened as the skies darkened. An unknown male teacher lifted me up in his arms; I went limp and relaxed, feeling rescued—I was indeed safe—protected. The red cape was already beginning to warm my freezing, bare flesh. However, I was emotionally scarred by the trauma of being utterly and hopelessly lost, but I would always remember the warmth of the cape and the sheer relief of being found.

Engraved in my mind remained the striking contrast of the pure white snow and the deep red cape. Later in life, this frightful event and this colored image would come to mean something of greater importance—it would fill my life with a much deeper meaning . . . but for now, I was still a young girl lost in a world filled with uncertainty and a home filled with impending danger . . .

Chapter Three

ATTACK ON INNOCENCE

Taken

This day was unexpected—I was at least fourteen years old, and still in Walford Secondary Modern School. Mother must have gone out, along with all my siblings. For whatever the reason, I was home alone with my father. As a teenager, I had successfully avoided and resisted his lustful advances and thought the sexual abuse was over. I was grossly mistaken. This day was different and would mark the worst event of his depraved, sexual crimes.

Due to the extreme trauma of what happened, there is a blank in my memory. Emotionally, I believe I just shut down, so I do not recall how I was in my parents' upstairs bedroom, but my father had taken me in there. Neither do I recollect how I was forced onto their double bed.

The brutal attack began with being pinned down, my hands held tightly beside both sides of my head. Overwhelming hysteria from the depths of my inner being produced tears that welled up and overflowed down my anxious face. As I was unable to hold them in, the tears just continued to stream, while I tried desperately to control the surmounting fear.

Faint whimpers broke the otherwise dead silence. I always stayed silent during his sexual abuse—to cry out might anger him more. I tried really hard to be quiet, but this time I could not control the flow of tears or the release of slight sobs. In my confused mind, I questioned, reasoning . . . *He had never become physically aggressive, so why would he not let me go?* I was helpless . . . his sheer weight and strength held me down. Why was my father on top of me this time? There was no escape from his controlling grip. All I continued to do was cry.

Then, after what seemed to be an endless amount of time, Father glared at me so angrily—disgusted, even frustrated, with my tears and helpless whimpers. Unbeknownst to me at the time, he had failed in his attempt to sexually assault me. So, he released his sordid grip, and allowed me to get up; with an angry scowl, he told me, "GET OUT!" Thankful for freedom, without another second to lose, I immediately left my parents' bedroom, still silently crying and traumatized by what had just happened.

Suicide

Immediately, and without a second thought, I went downstairs to the kitchen and reached for my mother's painkillers, tranquillizers, valium and other strong medications. I just grabbed any bottle and stood motionless . . . suicide. In that one moment, everything from the past surfaced; the years and years of sexual abuse came crushing to the forefront of my adolescent life. I had reached a massive peak—a breaking point. I could not take this anymore. I just wanted the torment to stop. Death would stop everything. He could never harm me again; death was an escape—the only way out.

Still motionless, I dangled in indecision between life and death . . . the attack had pushed me mentally to the edge of a cliff—a sheer precipice. I stared aimlessly into the bottomless abyss. Death seemed a sharp drop into the unknown. Yet, I had a greater fear of death than I had of my father, and as I struggled within my mind, the battle of extreme thoughts continued. I still contemplated suicide as an escape from my tormenter, but suddenly my thoughts were interrupted; I heard movement upstairs.

Escape

Raging fear gripped me once more. *Would I be attacked again?* The fear of death suddenly switched to a stronger sense of survival—I wanted to live. Adrenalin rushed through my weakened body still in shock. I had been stilled in motion, like a rabbit caught in an oncoming car's headlights.

His upstairs movements jolted me like a needed slap in the face; the fear of my father caused me to spring into action. In an instant, the pills that would have caused my death were dropped, and I ran towards the old, heavy, back kitchen door. Desperately, I cried to myself, *Open! Please open!*

To my horror, the door would not budge. Frantically pulling at the door, a thought darted into my mind . . . *The door is locked from the inside, and I will need the key to escape!*

Quickly, my mind grasped the unfolding scenario, as if putting clues together that unlocked a murder mystery. Father had locked me in; he had planned my assault. Realizing his plan, I was thrown emotionally into a fearful frenzy of uncontrollable terror. This had become a house of horrors—a locked prison—and I, his prisoner, had to get out!

I moved to the next small, back room and tried the French glass doors that opened into the back garden. They too were locked. Panic stricken, I knew the only way out would be to reach the front door before my father saw me and would try to stop me. From his bedroom, the stairs were only a short distance, and they led straight to the front door—my only place left I could go to escape.

My thoughts and feet reacted in unison . . . I opened the inside door that led to the short hallway; trying to calm my mind, I said to myself, *Just a short distance to run before I reach the front door to freedom.* But fear had caused a clumsy numbness, my feet felt like heavy weights, and, as I ran, I seemed to move in slow motion.

Reaching the front door and not looking back, afraid to see the face of my attacker, I fumbled desperately at the door knob—twisting and twisting, but it would not open. I clumsily fiddled with the small center lock to release the door. Still, it remained securely shut.

Feeling a sense of dread and hopelessness in my escape, I happened to glance upward—this door had also been bolted from the inside by a small, gold chain and a second bolt higher up. Relieved I did not need a key, I hastily released them both. This time I tried the handle one more time . . . it opened . . . at last I was free!

Fresh air hit my face, and I screamed the loudest, bloodcurdling scream ever . . . but there was no voice to this scream; it had come from deep within. It was as if my very soul, my inward being, had suffered a tremendous wound and screamed out in immense pain. Have you ever heard a soul scream? I believe I have—my own. I had heard it with my own ears, but I cannot fully explain or understand the phenomena. For a moment, in shock—I felt like I stood between reality and unreality.

Outside, everything looked like a captured, still picture frozen in time—the deep blue sky and the fluffy, white clouds, with brilliant light from the warm summer sun against quaint solid brick houses, along with perfectly kept gardens, where our friendly neighbors lived. Nothing moved, and there was not a soul about to call for help. As if bringing me back to life, a gentle breeze blew against my numb face;

I took in a deep breath and filled my lungs with the fresh air.

Momentarily, still numb with shock, my thoughts turned to the prison door now wide open. Quickly I ran out and headed towards the short, white, front garden gate—the last blockade to my freedom. As I released the simple latch, I felt strength surging back into my legs and bolted full force. It felt good to run and feel the blood pumping throughout my whole body. The warm summer breeze flung back my streaming tears, and they mingled with my long, curly hair, flowing in the wind.

A Cry For Help

I safely reached the home of my best friend and schoolmate. I immediately found comfort in her friendship and readily told her what had happened. In this familiar home, perhaps I would find safety and help. With the silence of my sexual abuse broken, I felt so alleviated—finally, I had told someone and the hidden secret was out. I only wanted what was happening to stop, no other consequences, no drama.

The family convened; I heard faint voices talking privately while I was in the other room. After some time passed, I became painfully aware of their final decision. They were not going to call the police; in fact, they thought it best not to get involved at all. They were sympathetic, of course, and let me stay for a few hours, but eventually, I had to return to the house from which I had escaped.

My father was right after all. I had spoken out when I was on the edge of breaking. I had told someone I trusted when I could not take the violation anymore. But I had come to a home that gave me the impression that it was not their business—that what happens behind closed doors should remain private. They had taken a broom and swept away the dirty matter, all the ugly details of my sexual abuse hidden right under their own carpet.

Disheartened, and yet resigned to return, I had to go home. At least Mother would be home and dinner would be waiting. On my arrival, family life continued the same, business as usual; except, I noticed, we all sat around the dinner table in an awkward silence—as if nothing ever happened. Had my friend's parents called my home? Had my father explained away the situation?

It was not until later, when I was older, that I fully understood how very close I came to being violently raped by my own father. After that teenage trauma, the nightmares came . . . I was always trying in slow motion to run for the door—always trying to get out and escape.

Far From Innocence

Independence in England came at an early age; most kids left school at the age of sixteen and home by eighteen. Work was ingrained in our young lives early, and at eleven years old, I had gotten my own paper round.[33] I often took my youngest sister with me, because she had the sweetest, angelic face, and whenever I took her, we got far more tips.

Later, I gained more experience working different Saturday jobs: at the local sweet shop,[34] waitressing, a local hairdressing shop in the town of Hayes and working in the haberdashery[35] department in a large Ealing store in the Broadway shopping center. Elated by my new earnings, I excitedly bought the clothes I wanted—modern fashions and cute shoes—finally, no more hand-me-downs!

Once school finished, I really was not sure what I wanted to do with my life. My father often said it is always good to learn a trade; he was the one who actually suggested hairdressing as an occupation. I nervously went for an interview and was soon accepted to work full-time at a local hairdressing shop in the town of Hayes. While working as an apprentice, I was sent to Hounslow College to gain my City and Guilds[36] in cosmetology. I thrived there and won a first place award in a hairdressing competition.

During my final years in Walford Secondary Modern School, I had developed a close friendship with a wonderful, young man. As we grew up together,

---

[33] paper round: British term for paper route.

[34] sweet shop: a store that sells chocolate, cigarettes and often newspapers.

[35] haberdashery: cloth, pins, thread, etc. used for sewing, or a shop or a department of a large store that sells these items.

[36] City and Guilds: vocational education organization in the United Kingdom founded on November 11, 1878, by the City of London and 16 Livery (trade) companies.

he became endearingly known as "the boy who lived just around the corner." I continued my relationship with him throughout two years of college. He was both a companion and confidant— he knew all about my father's sexual abuse. While I was with him, Father kept his distance. I ignored his sexual comments and innuendos and stayed away from home as much as possible.

He was my first real love. I was attracted to his dark eyes and dead, straight hair which made him look very Asian. He reminded me of my idol at the time, Bruce Lee—whose picture was plastered all over my side of the bedroom wall—except my boyfriend was a little shorter and, of course, not so muscular.

It was to this young man that I lost my virginity. In his home, while his parents were in the back room watching television, we were secretly having sex in the front room, while supposedly watching television. Even though his parents would often go to the bathroom and check on us from time to time, the light from their room, when they opened their door, acted as our quick alert.

I had no moral guidance, as far as sex went, from my mother, and Father had awakened me to sexual experiences. So I was terribly unprepared for relationships in general and muddled through on my own. Anyway, by this time, most of my school friends were already in sexual relationships. They were the ones who came alongside and educated me on what to do. They introduced me to a free family planning clinic, where I was able to be placed on the pill. I was no longer a virgin, and I wanted to do my best to protect myself against teenage pregnancy.

Having a steady boyfriend meant taking holidays together. It was the norm in English society for parents to allow their teenage daughters and their boyfriends to go on trips together; nobody would bat an eyelid.[37] So, in the summer, I went on a holiday to the Isle of Wight with my boyfriend, staying in our own caravan[38] near the Isle's beautiful, sandy beaches.

This romance was magical. One day I would be married to him so I thought, as the date was set, but it was not meant to be. I did not know the reason why he had changed his mind. Perhaps his friends dissuaded him? Or did he find it too hard to handle my sordid, past? Mother said it was due to being too beneath him. I was not good enough; I was a commoner, but so was he. I never knew . . . hurt and rejected, I set my eyes elsewhere.

It wasn't long before I met another young man. He was older, a friend of my brothers. He was tall, ruggedly handsome with a head of thick, curly hair. He instantly filled the emptiness of my heart, and I

---

[37] bat an eyelid: to show no signs of distress even when something shocking is said or done.
[38] caravan: a wheeled vehicle for living or traveling in, especially for holidays, that contains beds and cooking equipment. A caravan can be pulled by a car.

often found myself waiting and longingly looking for him from an upstairs window, just to get a glimpse of him walking down the street towards our home. The relationship quickly became sexual. This time, it was my parents who allowed us to be left alone in an upstairs bedroom.

Another summer came. With my eldest brother and his girlfriend, we rented a home in Wales to enjoy a holiday. Castles were explored and we hiked many hills and valleys; other times, we rented bikes to reach the distant, little villages. Evenings were spent reading the famous *Hobbit* book. At this time of my life, I was thoroughly happy.

Soon holiday time was over; we were home and back into the routine of everyday work life. The local pubs were our regular hangouts to drink, play cards and shoot pool.

One evening, not able to hold my liquor well, I made such a ridiculous spectacle of myself; I had gone up to a bloke[39] and slapped him in the face. Irate[40] and teaching me a good lesson, he slapped me hard, right back. I have never been so embarrassed in my whole life, but that is what happens when you drink—it makes such a fool out of you.

---

[39] bloke: a man, a fellow or guy.
[40] Irate: feeling or characterized by great anger.

In fact, one time, drinking almost cost me my life! I had no intentions of dying; I was just having a grand old time with a young co-worker and her boyfriend. That night at her home, she handed me some pills, secondals.[41] Foolishly I took them—I had never taken drugs before, and I was unaware of the dangers of this lethal cocktail of alcohol and drugs. The mixture knocked me out. Was there ill intent? I would never know.

The next thing I remember was waking up in a hospital room, hooked up to an IV. The doctor explained that I could have died from alcohol poisoning. My friends had called 999 for an ambulance. Later, when back at work, my co-worker told me that she and her boyfriend, after I took the mixture of alcohol and secondals, had heard me choking as I lay unconscious. A thick, black mucous had collected in my throat, and her boyfriend had to make a hook with his finger to pull it out—he had saved my life.

Father came to pick me up from the hospital. As strange as this may seem, he was still my dad. I felt ashamed, and I could see the worry on his face . . . I had caused him pain and humbly apologized. He never condemned me, never yelled, we just drove home in silence, and I sat there awkwardly with nothing else to say for myself.

---

[41] secondals: barbiturate, hypnotic, used as a sleeping aid or to calm a person before surgery.

Glad to place the incident behind me, I continued on with my new relationship. Soon, unexpectedly, I was given an ultimatum by my parents—break up with my boyfriend or leave home. I left home. My attachment to him was much stronger, enough to break my mother's heart, but she had never known how unsafe home was for me. How glad I was to finally get out . . .

For a time, we lived together with an older co-worker of mine. Then, young and deeply in love, I was married at the age of 20, September 29, 1979, in a quaint, old, brick church in Northolt Village.

Chapter Four

RESTORED INNOCENCE

What Man Is This?

As a happy newlywed, I nestled down in a new, shared home with my sister-in-law in Chiswick, London. One day, during the Easter season while home alone, I decided to watch an old movie that was on television, *Jesus of Nazareth*.[42] The actor, Robert Powell, who portrayed Christ, had large, clear, pool-like eyes that seemed to look right through me. He captured my attention completely.

A dramatic and intense scene began—an adulterous woman in open shame was thrown down publicly in front of Jesus for judgment . . . stones in the hands of her accusers were ready to be hurled at her until she was dead. Jesus stood between her and the stones . . . I noticed the writing in the sand, the wisdom of His words, His commanding authority, as one by one the stones of judgment were dropped, along with their railing accusations. I was somehow drawn to this Man, and, within myself I wondered, "What Man is this?"

---

[42] *Jesus of Nazareth:* one of Christ's earthly titles; Nazareth located in lower Galilee is the well traveled home town, of His mother Mary, and Joseph who was a carpenter.

I identified with the adulterous woman—her shame, guilt and uncleanness. To a guilt-ridden woman, who sank in shame at His feet, Jesus asked "Where are your accusers?" She replied, "No one, Lord." Unforgettable words to a sinner were uttered by her Lord, "Neither do I condemn you." Then with her sins forgiven, He simply commanded her, "Go and sin no more."

Through this humble, yet majestic Man, her eyes and heart became open spiritually. For the first time in her empty life, this Man had reached out to her with His everlasting love . . . and, although not fully realized, my life had been touched too. I am sure that her love for this Man, Jesus her Rescuer, became evident, as she would follow Him, deeply devoted to her Lord and Savior, for the rest of her life.

As the wonderful story of Jesus' life unfolded before my eyes, I saw this innocent Man, after doing so much good, betrayed, forcefully arrested and unfairly questioned by Jewish leaders. After they were finished with Him, they led Him to Pilate, who turned Him over to cruel, Roman soldiers. They brutally tortured and mercilessly whipped Him beyond all human recognition—He was beaten to a pulp.

Ruthlessly, they placed a crown of thorns upon His already bloodied head. Finally, they sentenced Him to be crucified on a wooden cross . . . a cross He carried on His painful, open, flesh-shredded back.

As I began to contemplate Christ, I sat there silently weeping . . . weeping along with all the other women who had wailed and screamed out for His freedom. He was innocent! The scenes were incredibly moving . . . the film ended with Jesus' resurrection. Happy that it ended well and without giving it another thought, I carried on with my mundane, ordinary, English life.

A New Journey

In God's divine providence, my ordinary life would soon change. A lost relative's telephone number had been found. A call was quickly made that reunited a separated family. It had been twenty years since Alfred Engeron, my father-in-law, had been seen or heard from. Divorced from my English mother-in-law, he lived in his own native country—America, and before we knew it, we were invited to go stay with him. Breaking my mother's heart again, I gladly set off for a new adventure, unfeeling towards her maternal pain.

As the airplane came in for the landing, the sky cleared and the view from the window showed me a new land. Vast, mountainous territory spanned in every direction, and as we got closer, I could see the streets were all basically straight—very different from England's curvy and winding roads.

Alfred met us at the Los Angeles International Airport. He was a tall, burly man, like a lumberjack.

Louisiana was his home state, and I was told he was a Cajun.[43] I was soon to find out that he was the best cook, making all his sauces from scratch. His recipes were spicy—jambalaya, shrimp creole and meat balls in spaghetti sauce—which, quite frankly, this English girl, who cooked bland food, wasn't used to.

Alfred gave us a warm and generous welcome; his actions showed us a real and genuine love. As we drove away from the airport, I felt happy to leave behind the hustle and bustle of people crowding along the drab, grey concrete streets of Los Angeles city. I am not much of a city girl, and felt much more at home as our destination took us through the beautiful suburbs. Once out of the city, I stared wide-eyed as I viewed California for the first time. The radiant, summer sun, tall, swaying palm trees and majestic mountains that surrounded us left me completely awestruck!

Outwardly, my new father-in-law was somewhat gruff, but to me, he would become a gentle giant, fondly known as Dad. He was a father figure—strong and protective. Truly, he cared for this young, English girl, his daughter-in-law, now in a foreign country, so far away from family and friends. His was the first welcome; his was the first embrace into his country, his home and his heart.

---

[43] Cajun: a member of any of the largely self-contained communities in the bayou areas of southern Louisiana formed by descendants of French Canadians, speaking an archaic form of French.

Unbeknownst to us, Alfred, my father-in-law, had become a Christian in 1979, the same year I had married his son. He told me that once he became a believer he had burnt his books on witchcraft and poured all of his strong alcohol down the drain. He had been a staunch Catholic, but was now a fiery Christian, boldly sharing his faith.

Being a rather nosey and curious person, when he had gone to work, I opened the small doors of his front room cabinet. On the shelves were piles of Christian tracts and Gospel comic books written by Chick Publications. These simple-to-read tracts were graphically illustrated. They didn't beat about the bush, and each tract had a straightforward, hard-hitting message—turn or burn! Just what this common English girl needed!

I momentarily reflected back to the movie, *Jesus of Nazareth*. Just months earlier, during Easter, I had sat alone, quietly watching and weeping about this Man. I had contemplated His reality . . . "What Man is this?" Now, through these tracts, they showed that Jesus was the only One who could save me.

I had been unaware of God's existence, but at that point, after reading these tracts, all I knew was that I was a sinner going to hell. The Spirit of God had convicted me.

My husband returned home from work and later that evening, I asked if he wanted to say the simple sinner's prayer in the back of one of the Christian tracts. I wanted to accept Jesus into my heart. My husband willingly joined me by our bedside. It was the fear of God and punishment in hell that drove me to my knees that night. I had made a sincere decision to accept the Lord as my Savior on October 1980. There weren't any fireworks or bursts of emotion that day, but the next day . . . when I awoke, I had an immense sense of joy and an insatiable thirst for God's Word. I was a sponge soaking in the Word of God like water. A true change had taken place in my life . . .

Words are very powerful; the truth of that statement is found in Proverbs 18:21: *Death and life are in the power of the tongue* . . . Throughout my childhood, words from my father brought torment, anguish, mental suffering and a cruel bondage that chained me to him for years. My father's words and actions had almost caused my death; I was driven by them to thoughts of suicide. In contrast, words from the Bible are living and gave me life—a spiritual awakening and an incredible freedom.

Free . . . oh, as a child, how I loved to run free . . . and now I *was* truly free! As a newborn thirsts for their mother's milk, so this new thirst for God's Word began to govern my life.

White As Snow

While making exciting new discoveries in Scripture, I read this life-changing verse: *Therefore, if anyone is in Christ, he is a new creation; old things have passed away; behold, all things have become new* (2 Corinthians 5:17).

I don't know if there are any human words to describe the elation, the deep, immense happiness I was feeling. For me, as a little girl who had gone through so much abuse at the hands of her father, and then as an adolescent who had led a sinful life, these words from the Bible meant everything. Gone was my past life! Gone were the chains of childhood suffering, the prison where I was afflicted mentally and suffered emotional abuse. Gone was the shame, along with the heavy weight of responsibility for the secrecy I had carried! Gone was my promiscuous adolescence! I had a brand new life—a new beginning in Christ—all happening in a new country, America!

Silently I read the Bible before God. He spoke to me through His Word, as if I had been whispered to by God Himself . . . in the inner depths of my human soul: *"Come now, and let us reason together,"* says the LORD, *"Though your sins are like scarlet,[44] they shall be as white as snow; though they are red like crimson,[45] they shall be as wool . . ."* (Isaiah 1:18).

---

[44] scarlet: a cloth, doubled dipped in red dye; a stain incapable of being removed—crimson.
[45] crimson: a red dye made from the dried, crushed bodies of the adult Kermes Vermilio insect; a crimson grub and its connection to the color red, used to dye clothing.

This Scripture revealed to me, a vivid colored mystery that scarlet and crimson represented the irremovable stains of sin, now washed white as snow by the cleansing blood of Jesus; as the pure wool of an innocent lamb.

Certainly, that Scripture was descriptive of me—my sins were, indeed irremovable as scarlet. By biblical standards, they were red as crimson. Before marriage, I had lived a life of immoral fornication enjoying its sinful pleasures. For years, I had continued to live with the shameful stain of my father's sinful lust—an irremovable stain that so drenched my soul in guilt and disgrace. I felt impure, dirty and used. Surely this sordid mark would remain with me my entire life.

This Scripture brought an instantaneous flood of childhood memories . . . back to the little lost schoolgirl, numbed by cold in the snowy woods protected and covered by a red cape.

I began to reason the meaning of the *white snow*—purity. *Can God remove such deep irremovable stains that mark a sinner's life and make them white as snow? Was there any hope of freeing me from these sins that bound me into an eternity of fire and judgment? What could take away years of shame, guilt and impurity placed on me by my father?*

My pondering thoughts continued to uncover such deep mysteries. There is another passion, unlike the sinful passion of lust that leaves behind the irremovable crimson stain of sin. Christ's passion stemmed from a redemptive[46] love so deep, that His red blood ran freely from His broken and bruised body. Jesus willingly became crushed by cruel crucifixion. His red blood shed on the cross proved to me His pure, holy passion—His love was freely given. I had now believed and received His sacrifice for the forgiveness of my sins to have my deepest sins removed. Only the cleansing blood of Jesus could remove the stain of sin on my life and make me white as snow!

I thought about the pure, powder-white snow on the hard, frozen ground. White snow identified to me clearly that by Jesus' blood, the soiled, sinful slate of my life was indeed wiped clean; my sins were completely erased and washed away. Before Him, I was pure as the white driven snow. I had never felt pure . . . instead I had wandered aimlessly in this world, seemingly with no real purpose except to be some man's whore—yet God's love made me pure and innocent, as white snow . . .

---

[46] redemptive: a release effected by payment of ransom. God's effective work of grace; the purchasing of a sinner from the debt of sin, through Jesus Christ blood shed on the cross.

Lost And Found

My thoughts returned to contemplate the meaning of the red cape. I had experienced the fears of being lost, wandering and wondering if I were going to die. The vivid red cape, lovingly wrapped about my body as I felt its warmth and protection, kept me from the deathly, biting cold. I felt the relief of being found safe and secure, as I was lifted out of all danger by the strong arms of an unknown, male schoolteacher.

This experience had given me an amazing and rich comparison for being spiritually lost and found. I still felt so much like this little, lost girl, stained with my own scarlet sin; but now I knew I was found by my Savior. He became my strong-armed Deliverer who lifted me out of my world of danger.

The vivid, blood red cape will always represent the shed blood of Christ, the Man who laid down His life for me. He won the victory on the cross and, in His love, wrapped His arms securely around me. Christ's strong arms have lifted me out of death—hell's torturous pit. I look forward to being safe with Him in heaven's home—His promised place in eternity. By His strength and grace,[47] I can live joyfully in this world, often so spiritually cold, dark and frightening.

---

[47] grace: is God's unmerited, unearned favor extended freely to sinners; God's riches at Christ's expense.

These spiritual, contrasting images of truth are engraved on my heart and mind forever! I was sinful as crimson and, by God's grace, made white as snow—utterly lost and joyfully found and protected by Christ's precious blood. As I reasoned, the mystery of the Gospel message became clearly understood. *Amazing Grace*, an old hymn I had sung as a child in school, flooded into my mind:

Amazing Grace

Amazing grace! How sweet the sound
That saved a wretch like me!
I once was lost, but now am found;
Was blind, but now I see.
'Twas grace that taught my heart to fear,
And grace, my fears relieved;
How precious did that grace appear
The hour I first believed.

Through many dangers, toils and snares
I have already come;
'Tis grace has brought me safe thus far,
And grace will lead me home.

The Lord has promised good to me,
His Word my hope secures;
He will my Shield and Portion be,
As long as life endures.

Yea, when this flesh and heart shall fail,
And mortal life shall cease,
I shall possess, within the veil,
A life of joy and peace.

When we've been there ten thousand years,
Bright shining as the sun,
We've no less days to sing God's praise
Then when we've first begun.

Amazing grace, how sweet the sound,
That saved a wretch like me.
I once was lost but now am found,
Was blind, but now I see.

Written by John Henry Newton
(Between 1760-1770)

Now, looking through spiritual eyes, so many more things from my childhood have become crystal clear. I realize, although hidden to me at the time, God was always there—His holy handprints were completely interwoven throughout the pages of my childhood life. He had just been invisible.

The Baptist Church, with its huge, wooden cross that hung before me as I swung on the swings; the school memorization of what is commonly known as *The Lord's Prayer*; the Christmas carols and beautifully written hymns I had sung in every English school I attended—all held a Christian truth.

Everything flooded my awakened and thankful heart with rich, new meaning. I now know the God who hung on the rugged cross; the God for whom these Christmas carols and old hymns were written and sung—the God of the Bible—my God!

Yet, another childhood song came to mind. *All Things Bright and Beautiful,* one of the very first songs I had learned about God our Creator . . .

All Things Bright and Beautiful

All things bright and beautiful,
All creatures great and small,
All things wise and wonderful:
The Lord God made them all.

Each little flower that opens,
Each little bird that sings,
God made their glowing colors,
And made their tiny wings.

The purple-headed mountains,
The river running by,
The sunset and the morning
That brightens up the sky.

The cold wind in the winter,
The pleasant summer sun,
The ripe fruits in the garden,
God made them every one.
God gave us eyes to see them,

And lips that we might tell
How great is God Almighty,
Who has made all things well.

Written by Cecil Frances Alexander (1848)

Salvation

Everything was well with me; I had salvation—I was a lost sinner saved from hell. I understood now that nothing in my life had happened by coincidence. Jesus had pursued me in England, and, in His providence, I had come to America where I read and understood the Gospel. He led me like a Shepherd by His grace to a wonderful place—the foot of the cross, and a miracle had taken place. You see, Jesus had also seen what had happened in my childhood—everything: the sexual abuse, the near rape, and my young life without God and without hope in this world—He saw it all.

Yet, willingly, Jesus made loving provision for my healing and salvation. He alone understood my suffering, because He had suffered. As I was taken as an innocent victim, so was He taken as an innocent victim, unlawfully abducted and arrested during the night. As an innocent child, I remained silent in the face of my abuser. Christ, an innocent Man, remained silent in the face of His abusers. The Word of God tells us—*He was oppressed and He was afflicted, yet He opened not His mouth; He was led as a lamb to the slaughter, and as a sheep before its shearers is silent, so He opened not His mouth* (Isaiah 53:7). Truly, Jesus was as silent as a lamb, the Lamb of God, who takes away the sins of the world.

I had been my father's prisoner; I had silently chosen to take the abuse, so that my family could stay together. Jesus, hands bound, knew what it was like to be a prisoner and, for my sake, didn't seek an escape. He willingly died so I could remain with Him forever—for all eternity.

The friend's home I turned to for help didn't offer any assistance; they didn't want to get involved. Pilate, a Roman Governor, could have released Jesus, but he was swayed by the crowds; he offered Him no help. Fearing man, Pilate didn't want to get involved; he listened to those who wanted an innocent man crucified and washed his hands of Christ's innocent blood (Matthew 27:24).

I suffered the tremendous weight and torment of sexual and emotional abuse; He suffered torturous physical and emotional abuse. He was mocked, spit on, beaten and bruised—crushed! I had suffered immensely, but He had agonized so much more—oh yes, He understood my pain!

Much later, as I studied, I came to understand that Jesus identified himself with an insignificant worm: *But I am a worm, and no man; a reproach of men, and despised by the people* (Psalm 22:6). According to the Hebrew, the word *worm* in this passage has the same meaning as *crimson* in Isaiah 1:18—the irremovable red stain that is produced when the worm is crushed.

Astonishingly, as Christ was crushed, like that worm, His red blood removed the irremovable crimson stain of my sin. By His blood I am cleansed!

Jesus was not only physically crushed; He had the weight of the world's sin on His shoulders to carry . . . and all for love . . . He alone—by His blood—could remove our sin, once and for all.

So you see, Jesus understood how I felt—how other abused victims feel. He too will meet them at the cross . . . Jesus will meet every person in their deepest need at the cross.

Nightmares still came, but I learned to pray when those things happened, and in time, they faded away. With Christ I had no therapy, no hang-ups, I didn't need counseling, I didn't need a support group; in fact, at the time, I wasn't even in a church. For me, God just met me . . . I was led by the Holy Spirit Himself to the cross, to Jesus . . . to God, as He was the only One who could heal me where no mortal man could ever touch . . . Jesus was enough.

Future And Hope

Thank God, I never went through with my attempt to commit suicide. I praise Him for intercepting my life at twenty! Oh, His wonderful plans I would have missed—the pure joys He had designed for my future! God's Word promises us a future and a hope: *For I know the plans I have for you, says the Lord. They are plans for good and not for evil, to give you a future and a hope* (Jeremiah 29:11,TLB). I had a whole new direction for my life, as God took me by His hand and . . . *brought me out of a horrible pit, out of the miry clay, and He set my feet upon a rock, and established my steps* (Psalm 40:2).

Jesus is the Rock, and in Him, I found the stability I needed. I found love, true love, in my humble Savior, who loved me enough to even die for me. One of my favorite Bible verses says: ". . . *Yes, I have loved you with an everlasting love; therefore with lovingkindness I have drawn you*" (Jeremiah 31:3).

My husband and I, began attending Calvary Chapel West Covina, with Pastor Raul Ries. The church was walking distance from the Sunset Crest Apartments, where we lived. Here I witnessed true Christian love—a contagious love, warm and accepting; a Christ centered worship, as one or two persons played harmoniously with a simple guitar; and line upon line teaching—a sound teaching of God's Word by our pastor.

I had come from England, a land known in times past for its rich, Christian heritage. Yet, sadly I had not heard the Gospel in my own country. This land had once professed Christianity, but, from what I saw and experienced, it was nothing more than plain, old tradition and pompous religiosity. The Church there is, even today, obviously, as dead as a doornail.[48] Yet, here in America, I had come to know the Gospel and the truth of a personal relationship with Jesus Christ.

---

[48] dead as a doornail: an ancient phrase from 1350. Believed to get its meaning from a process of clenching—a hammered nail was driven through and the protruding end bent over to secure it. This may be why the nail was referred to as being 'dead'.

Chapter Five

GOD GIVEN CLOSURE

Forgiveness

As a little girl, forgiveness was an unknown, foreign and alien word to me—in my family it was never used, nor mentioned. On no occasion was it taught or spoken; forgiveness basically did not exist. I cannot remember saying a simple, "sorry" to any of my siblings to make things right. I remember the spankings though! In a British, *stiff-upper-lipped* society, you were taught not to cry and it was more familiar to hold hurts in, to never address them, and to go on like nothing ever happened. That is exactly how I handled my sexual abuse; bravely, with no emotion. The abuse was just buried deep down inside me. I had gone forward in life, as if it never happened.

Jesus had become my Savior, and, as I began to know Him more intimately, He also became my Wonderful Counselor. As a brand new Christian, while I was reading my Bible and praying, the Lord spoke to me about forgiveness through a very familiar passage, *The Lord's Prayer*. I had read this as a young girl, having been taught in school to recite these verses from memory. My little sisters and I had created our own made-up tune to these verses, which, at the time, were meaningless. How terribly sad to have to say that, but now, for me, The Lord's Prayer has taken on more meaning than *heaven n' earth!*[49]

I read this portion of the prayer with my spiritual eyes now open and my mind full of understanding:

> *And forgive us our debts, as we forgive our debtors. For if you forgive men their trespasses, your heavenly Father will also forgive you. But if you do not forgive men their trespasses, neither will your Father forgive your trespasses.*
>
> MATTHEW 6:12, 14, 15

I inquisitively questioned within myself: *"I wonder who I can forgive Lord?"* . . . and in a still small voice, it came to me . . . *my father . . . the one who, by his lust and strength, crushed me—an innocent child—with his constant, sexual abuse.* He had created within me a tremendous fear and brought me, at one point, to the edge of suicide. His offence of sexual abuse was to be dealt with early in my walk with the Lord. I believe God did not allow the abuse to remain hidden in my past, as it would have placed a damper[50] on my brand new Christian walk. It truly was a work of the Holy Spirit, teaching me about forgiveness.

---

[49] heaven n'earth: it is above and beyond the limited human knowledge contained only in just the earth's heaven and land.

[50] damper: to have a dulling or numbing influence on something; to discourage, dishearten, deter, or depress the spirit.

I had encountered God . . . the Trinity—my heavenly Father, His Son and the Holy Spirit—my excellent Teacher, who expounded the wonders of forgiveness. As I studied, I learned that to be able to forgive, you need to know forgiveness, and to know Christ is to know forgiveness. This was a path to understanding—a revelation of forgiveness grasped in my own, new spiritual life. My soul had been freed from the crimson stains of my own sins, contrasted with the washing away of them and being made white as snow.

Having a clear understanding of my own wretchedness and receiving forgiveness for my own sins prepared me, on those holy grounds, to forgive others. Forgiveness became like a living stone in the foundation of my Christian walk. I had been so completely forgiven—my heart was made ready for the next important step . . . to forgive others. My response was that of an obedient child. Forgiveness was a spontaneous, natural and a freeing step of faith.

Obeying the prompting of the Holy Spirit and the direction of the Word of God, I nervously called my father in England. It was a difficult call, and after a brief, "Hello," I explained how I had become a Christian; then the words just came, "I forgive you, Dad." I explained to my father how he, too, could receive the same forgiveness for all the years of sexual abuse he had committed. Knowing that I had obeyed God's Word brought peace to my life; I had done my part—what mattered most was to be in right standing with God. I believe this act of obedience freed my life from bitterness, brought healing, and gave my father the gracious opportunity to repent and to receive salvation himself.

The response was unexpected and really sickening. I had to guard my heart from Father's twisted response. He excused himself by explaining that I had always been his favorite. Through secular counseling, he was made to believe that he was trying to love me, as in marriage. Such false counseling gave him a valid excuse for his behavior. Unable to wrap my head around that warped thinking, I instantly blurted out, "Love me?" How sick was his mind, how wrong was the counsel. "LOVE ME! Dad, you tried to rape me; you hurt me . . ." dead silence. He said no words of sorrow or remorse—nothing! The subject was changed, to what? I do not remember. Nonetheless I had forgiven him—I was free.

Ultimatums

My first two children were born consecutively. Sarah was born in 1981 and was dubbed the little *Gerber* baby. She grew into a darling child with big, beautiful, brown eyes, olive complexion, and she had a shy disposition. Although timid, she was bright and eager to learn.

These pleasant years enjoying motherhood were not without trials. Job loss, poverty and homesickness drove our growing family back and forth between

America and England. When we arrived home to England for the first time, Sarah was six months old. However, hearing of new job opportunities in America, we reconsidered our future and gave settling in America another try.

The day we left, my mother held Sarah tenderly in her arms. It would be another heart-wrenching goodbye. Our stay in England was long enough for my mother to form a strong attachment to her favored grandchild. A farewell gift of six adorable new dress outfits lay neatly in front of them. Mother was clearly in emotional distress; as tears rolled down her face, she lingered, staring down at her sweet grandchild's face, one last time, before reluctantly releasing Sarah to me. I knew mother would be robbed of the years in seeing her grandchild grow up; it pained me greatly.

David was born in 1983—he was chubby and cute. He developed into a curly, tote head—very blonde looking child—who was athletic and friendly, but at times, quite a handful. This young boy was full of energy—he always kept me on my toes. I became very well acquainted with the neighbors after he tussled with their children.

Back in America, steady work provided us a home and financial stability; however, it was not too much longer before another job loss crippled us financially. Alfred, my father-in-law, had tried to help us, but unable to stand on our own two feet and without waiting for the Lord to provide, we once again ran back to England.

Our family would provide the support and security we so desperately needed. In a plan to qualify for government housing, we didn't stay with family long; we had agreed to become homeless. Fortunately, we were able to apply for government housing by securing a place on an emergency housing list. While we waited, we lived in temporary housing at a hotel in Earl's Court, London. The plan paid off, and, after not too long of a wait, we landed a home in Radcliff Way, Northolt—which was not too far away from my mother or sisters. Our new three-bedroom home was on a corner lot, with a sizable fenced back garden for the children to play. As women do, I set about making our home into a cozy nest. Alfred kept in touch and kindly sent us Pastor Raul's sermons on tape. We began attending a small Baptist Church in Northolt. Sadly, as the months passed, after diligently attending church, we slowly fell into a backslidden state.

Then, on this one occasion, a tape with Pastor Raul Ries' Sunday sermon arrived with a message that changed the direction of our lives once more. It spoke about running away from the Lord to England, ironically the place we chose to find refuge. This time we had been in England for two whole years. Now phone calls and plans were being made by my husband without me, and, before I knew it, I was faced with an ultimatum—to remain in England or follow the man I had married back to America for a third time. It was a *fork in the road*; two very different paths lay before me, and a decision needed to be made. Twice we had tried to settle in America, and the ventures had miserably failed. Yet, here in England these last two years, I was more secure. In 1985, the direction for my life and my children's lives depended on what I would decide to do next . . .

Soon after, I had a vivid dream, and it got my full attention. God at times, spoke through dreams, just as He did with Joseph in the Bible. My dream compared two different scenes: in the first scene, I saw myself dancing with a dark stranger, and in the second, I was panic driven, shouting at the top of my lungs that Christ was coming! The earth shook and tall high-rise buildings were plummeting to the ground; people ran in every direction, not listening to my cry. In the middle of this terrible scenario was one of my beloved sisters—I had to save her! I awoke startled, with my heart beating rapidly and my face wet with tears—it had been so real!

I grabbed my Bible and randomly opened it, wanting the Lord to speak to me. I turned to Hebrews Chapter 10. As I read, I came across these God fearing verses:

For if we sin willfully after we have received the knowledge of the truth, there no longer remains a sacrifice for sins, but a certain fearful expectation of judgment, and fiery indignation which will devour the adversaries.

HEBREWS 10:26-27

Without a doubt, the dream, along with God's Word, gave me a strong warning from the Lord. I needed to repent of my backslidings and avoid willful sin; the consequences in these verses I read were just obvious. I could choose to dance with the devil, compromise and remain in England, or repent in godly fear and step into an unknown future. Broken and contrite, I gave my life fully back to the Lord—I chose the narrow path.

Then, with great difficulty, I had the task of telling my family that, once again, we would be leaving them to go back to America. As you can imagine, their response was unanimous! Everyone was firmly opposed to our decision. I could not speak to them of spiritual things, as they would not understand my reasoning, being natural men, not born of God's Spirit (1 Corinthians 2:14). My decision would seem sheer madness. My inner plight was hidden from them. So, in the end, I decided to share my strong Christian conviction in a simple statement—my family needed to be together.

An emotional tug of war ensued. My English family voiced their deep concerns the best they could. They knew our marriage had been struggling terribly for a while. I had returned from America the last time only weighing one hundred pounds and was a slim size three. I remember my oldest brother knocking on our front door yelling obscenities and telling me, if I left, I would come back to England in a box! He felt returning to America would be the death of me . . .

but I knew he was angry and spoke those things because he did not want to see his sister, nephew and niece leave. I am sure that he was generally concerned for our well-being.

My husband left for America first, so he could seek work before we would rejoin him; that was one of my conditions before I would uproot us all. Meanwhile, for accountability and spiritual support, I moved in with a large, Welsh family. The mother was a strong Christian, dedicated to principles and standards that would do the Puritans proud.

Mother and Father asked to be the ones to drive the children and myself to the airport. It was, in reality, their final ditch effort to persuade me to stay. The early morning was dismally dark; I had an early morning flight, and the sun had not yet risen. Father drove while Mother positioned herself to speak with me further.

Earnestly, she tried her best to convince me, "Stay—if you do, we shall help you." Pleading with her worldly wisdom, Mother persisted, "There are plenty more fish in the sea." Her words were tempting. It would be easy to walk away into a fresh, new beginning, but my commitment to the Lord was stronger. I was returning to Him, to Christ, not just back to America and the man awaiting me. Mother, seeing she had made no headway began to speak with a cruel bitterness that had entered her heart. "If you don't, I will never speak to you again!" That was her final ultimatum.

Leaving the car in silence, entering the airport and taking a seat on the plane was one of the hardest battles of my life. I had escaped all the pleading voices—the ultimatums that tore at my heart and emotions. I was left with a broken heart, ostracized from family, and feeling rejected and abandoned by those closest to me. I looked blankly out the plane window, ready to take off with my little darlings secure in the seats by me. With the plane in the air and England almost out of sight, I wondered at the possibility of ever returning to this familiar land. Unstoppable were the tears once again; I had held them back until I could no longer. The cost of following Christ was great. He was no longer Savior, but Lord—I had finally learned what it meant to take up my cross and follow Jesus. There was no turning back . . .

After arriving back in California in 1985, I went back to Calvary Chapel West Covina with Pastor Raul Ries—he was still preaching the Gospel. Although I was warmly welcomed by those who had known me previously, I felt like a little, black sheep, among the white, wooly ones attending church. It was then I was invited to attend a Women's Bible Study—now I would really grow as a Christian, learn to hear the voice of my Lord and Master, and be His devoted disciple.

Mother, however, was true to her word. Each time I called her, she simply hung up when she heard my voice—it would be twenty years before she had a change of heart and spoke with me. Yet, Jesus continued to comfort me with His words:

"He who loves father or mother more than Me is not worthy of Me. And he who loves son or daughter more than Me is not worthy of Me. And he who does not take his cross and follow after Me is not worthy of Me. He who finds his life will lose it, and he who loses his life for My sake will find it."

MATTHEW 10:37-39

As His disciple I could expect no different standard. Besides, Jesus had also said:

"Assuredly, I say to you, there is no one who has left house or brothers or sisters or father or mother or wife or children or lands, for My sake and the gospel's, who shall not receive a hundredfold now in this time—houses and brothers and sisters and mothers and children and lands, with persecutions— and in the age to come, eternal life."

MARK 10:29

Horrifically, while I remained in America, my father, without true repentance, committed the unthinkable. He continued to repeat his crimes by molesting his own granddaughters. All hell broke loose in my English family. I only kept in contact with my father for his birthday on 8 November, and during Christmas, by sending him cards and calling him to share the Gospel. Eventually, he moved further north of England and was living with a woman, who probably had no idea of his past. He told me that he had met some born-again Christians in his neighborhood; I urged him to listen to them. I knew God was graciously giving him yet another opportunity to accept Him. I stayed in touch with Father for about three years. Then silence . . . leaving me to wonder, *Had he died?* I would never know . . .

The Keepsake Letter

Mother . . . so many endearing thoughts and childhood memories exist from that one word. She was the central figure of our large family— six children who eagerly jostled for her love and attention. As a young woman, she had long, dark brown, wavy hair and dreamy, hazel-brown eyes that had such a remarkable sparkle. For an English woman, Mother had unblemished fair but olive skin; she looked more Italian and so did her dark, handsome brothers. Her youthful beauty reminded me very much of Elizabeth Taylor.

Years later, in the late summer of 2010, she sat before me—a frail figure of a once vibrant and beautiful woman. Her hair was still thick and wavy, but now short, white and silvery grey. Her neck was held in a supportive, cloth neck brace. In her nose, thin plastic tubes carried the needed oxygen to her failing lungs. Mother had cancer . . . it would take her life . . . I had flown from America to her home in England to be by her side. I prayed for the five, short days given to me, grateful for the time.

I wanted to take care of her, but she still, like a mother, wanted to take care of me. Off she went to the kitchen to make tea. As we sat together eating biscuits and sipping our strong, milky tea, we laughed, reminisced, and secretly, when she was not aware, I cried. Although unspoken, we both knew that this would be the last time we would have together, that eventually we would have to say our final goodbyes.

She still had that cheeky[51] twinkle in her eye and the often sarcastic, English sense of humor. Looking at me sideways, she asked me to turn off the oxygen. Removing the tubes, she brought to view the cancer-causing cigarette. She lit it up in front of me . . . I smiled, unsurprised.

"I already knew, Mother," I said. There was still too much evidence in the home that gave her away. The heavy, glass ashtrays and the smoky smell as I entered her home lingered everywhere. At this point, it wasn't worth fighting about; the cancer was incurable, and it wasn't like she was ever going to give up smoking. So she smoked often; afterwards, she took her inhaler and then went back on the oxygen.

Mother later allowed me to cut her thick hair, rub her aching back, make tea and sandwiches, and then bring to her a most favorite dessert—trifle![52]

---

[51] cheeky: impudent or irreverent character but typically in an endearing or amusing way.

[52] trifle: an English dessert made of custard, diced fruit interwoven with sponge fingers or more delicate spoke cake in jelly, topped with a layer of whipped cream and candy sprinkles.

She made sure my oldest brother took me out each day for a good meal.

The days were quickly passing, and as we talked, there was something she wanted to ask me. Mother needed closure to some questions that lingered from our past. Point blank, she stated, "I understand you have spoken to your father?" Mother had that authoritative tone in her voice. Her serious comment had caught me completely by surprise.

"Yes," I replied.

"Why?" she asked, with a lower, deepened tone.

Mother had divorced Father, because he had sexually abused his granddaughters. I knew what she was thinking, *Why on earth would I even talk to Father?* Such a man! He had ruined all of our lives; the hatred and bitterness ran deep through the veins of my mother's entire being.

However, despite my past, as far as I was concerned, my life was far from being ruined. I talked openly about my relationship with Jesus Christ . . . for once she listened; she usually started cussing at the mention of His name. I explained about forgiveness . . . a word unspoken in the Webster family. In simple words, I explained how I had been forgiven of my sins, and I had called Father to let him know that I had forgiven him.

An awkward silence followed; there was a deeper hurt yet to be uncovered—something she had held onto for all those years. Mother spoke from her broken heart, "Why did you write that you couldn't tell me because we weren't close?" She paused for a moment and sadly said, "I still have the letter in a drawer."

As she glanced at the old, wooden bureau[53] where the letter lay in one of its drawers, my mind instantaneously flashed back to thirty years before. I had written a letter to Mother telling her what had happened to me as a child. The letter was written in response to Father's plea of innocence, that he had not sexually abused his grandchildren. She had stood faithfully by my father until the letter arrived. The letter became a changing point—once read, she went from entire disbelief, to accepting the awful truth.

Devastated, she then made plans to divorce Father. Life would never be the same. Above that agonizing pain, was the one sentence in the letter that had shattered her heart. She had read how I couldn't confide in her; I couldn't go tell her the secret about Dad because we weren't close. I had no intentions of ever hurting my mother by writing the letter. I just wanted her to know the truth. I had wounded Mother and deeply so, but it wasn't the truth about Father that had hurt her so much; it was that one, uncaring statement, "We weren't close," that had caused her years upon years of emotional agony.

---

[53] bureau: a writing desk or writing table with drawers.

The letter was never crumpled up and thrown into a bin. Nor was it tossed into an open fire. No, it remained a keepsake letter. Unlike a hidden treasure of great value, it became a daily dagger to her heart—a painful reminder that she had failed as a mother. She had grappled with the thought that her eldest daughter didn't feel close enough to confide in her own mother concerning the terrible sexual abuse that had happened behind closed doors in her very own home. My words had brought so much grief that the letter remained in the bureau drawer, all these years.

A mother-daughter relationship is special; the bonds are strong and rarely unbreakable. I had broken a thread of that dear motherly bond, and it needed repair. As best as I could, I needed to make it right . . . gently and with contrition I said, "Mother, I was twenty and immature when that letter was written. I am older now and I am telling you, I will always be your close friend."

It seemed as if her burden was eased. The wrong, I hope, had been made right. I really can't remember saying, "Forgive me" or "Sorry, Mum." If I didn't, I should have.

Mother continued with deep regret in her voice over the past, "If only I had known, we could have all moved somewhere together. I was young enough then to have started over again." We remained sadly silent. Sounding even more heartbroken, she softly said, "I didn't know."

You see, many people, including a police constable, had accused her of knowing about the sexual abuse, but without hesitation, I answered, "I know, Mum. It wasn't your fault." I wanted to bring immediate relief from all the accusations that had haunted and condemned her all these years. Hoping to further ease her pain, I added, "Father was just evil. Even between sisters, we never knew what was happening to each other. He had us under so much fear that we were all quiet about it. Father was to blame, and if he didn't make it right before God, he would pay—he would go to hell."

With my explanation finished, she quickly quipped back, "Good!" and seemed happily vindicated.

Lightening the subject to a happier note, I asked, "So, Mother Dear, do you have any last words of wisdom for me? Last words are important, you know."

She smiled and the cheeky twinkle in her eyes was back. "Yeah, stop being such a Jesus freak!" We both burst into laughter, which lessened the intensity of the moment. Mother had thought I had gone off the deep end—off my rocker or been brainwashed in America. She had no understanding of what a personal relationship with Jesus Christ was, as she had been brought up with religious tradition.

Then sadly, as the five days were over, the morning came when I had to say goodbye. I hugged her tightly, lingering, finding it hard to let go. Focusing my eyes upon hers, I said softly, "Mother, you don't have to be afraid to die . . . just call on His Name." She knew of whom I spoke—Jesus. I continued on, hoping she would listen. "I will see you again; meet me under the tree of twelve fruits[54] in heaven."

I had done what I could . . . the rest I had to leave in God's loving hands. I can only hope that Mother listened to my life-giving words . . . I left for the airport, holding back the tears. I wanted to be strong for my mother . . . with her English pride still intact, I left her.

God had comforted my own breaking heart with a promise the night before, *"Today salvation has come to this house . . . for the Son of Man has come to seek and to save that which was lost"* (Luke 19:9-10). I was comforted knowing, that as Jesus had pursued me, He would make Himself known to Mother. He would be faithful to pursue her until her last, dying breath. I am sure she cried in private as she saw her eldest daughter leave—never to see me on earth again. That was the last time we spoke; she suffered and died the following June, shortly after her seventy-fourth birthday.

I pondered the passing of my mother and her generation. I felt like an orphan with no mother or father. Aunts, uncles and cousins either had passed

---

[54] tree of twelve fruits: Revelation 22:1-2 describes a tree that bears twelve different fruits, either side of a river, clear as crystal, that proceeds from the throne of God.

or remained out of touch, some because of distance. I now lived in America, and others, I am sure, stayed away when Father's sexual abuse was made public. As one brother put it, one day we had family, the next day we had no one—a huge rift separated us all. I found myself clutching to the memories of my fast-fading, English childhood days—life truly is brief.

Reflections

As a determined follower of Christ, I have served the Lord for over thirty-seven years. My life is fruitful and productive, as I remain on my narrow path with the Lord.

Pastor Raul, after much prayer and by faith, moved our church from West Covina, California to Diamond Bar, California; the new church is called Calvary Chapel Golden Springs. By God's providence, our growing family was able to follow.

Yet, trials came; sadly my marriage failed, perhaps, in part, due to my past. I would serve God single and with singleness of heart. The Lord is good and the blessings of the Lord continue. In my busy life are my four, grown children: Sarah, David, Victoria and Nathan. My eldest daughter, so far, has given me the joy of being a grandmother. I have three, rambunctious grandsons whom I adore.

Sometimes, I still ponder on the words given to my distraught mother and father by the English doctors. The death sentence—cystic fibrosis; four of us should have died young, but nobody ever did! Doctors were left baffled and scratching their heads, so to speak. They did not fully understand, as we had tested positive for the killer disease. The usual sweat tests to detect cystic fibrosis were completed. They concluded that it must have been a mutant gene, inactive in our system, yet not life threatening. I like to believe that God just had other master plans . . .

That shadow of death had always hung over me, but it fled, as Jesus, the Dayspring from on High, shined upon me. My fear of death was obliterated by His words of life. In Christ, I am promised an abundant life, as I journey as a pilgrim on this earth. After death, I have the hope of eternal life: *For God so loved the world that He gave His only begotten Son, that whoever believes in Him should not perish but have everlasting life* (John 3:16). I can look forward to a heavenly home with no more tears or pain—I'm not afraid to die . . .

Yet, ahead of me, there are more seasons of life to be enjoyed. Certainly, my life has blossomed and bloomed like an English, summer garden, full of the fragrances of life's pleasures and heartfelt joys.

As autumn brings a season of change, so, my life in this season seems to alter direction—like the golden-hued leaves blown everywhere in the cool autumn winds. I too am moved, into new ventures. This rich, colorful time of year brings together family and friends for Thanksgiving. God has left me with a thankful heart for all He has done and will do for me in the future.

Winter brings the jubilant message of the Gospel, when God left His Holy throne room to dwell among us. Each festive Christmas season, I reflect on the sweet memories of childhood days gone by.

Spring brings new life, like the earthbound caterpillar to the fluttering free flight of the butterfly, a living reminder each year of my transformation—a new life in Christ that has left me dancing in the rain once more . . .

As I recollect my childhood days, it is not the sexual abuse that overshadows the fond memories of growing up. It is not a shadow on my adult life either. I am clearly reminded of the streaming sunlight through the bay windows into the home where I grew up. Jesus, the Light of the world, has flooded streams of light that have penetrated the darkest places of my life. He has truly opened the window of understanding in my heart. I now bask in the Light of the Son who loves me and gave Himself for me. In that respect, I loved my childhood; I am thankful that this shadow of abuse never completely destroyed my childhood days. After all, you can't be afraid of a shadow; it's just a shadow.

An Invitation

Jesus, through the ages, has always extended a graceful invitation of salvation to all women in every nation of the world (John 4:9). Jesus loves women; the soul of a woman is priceless to Him, and her worth is far above rubies (Proverbs 31:10). He taught men that the treatment of women should be to love, cherish and honor them as the weaker vessel (Ephesians 5:25; 1 Peter 3:7). A man should provide for her needs physically, emotionally and spiritually (Ephesians 5:26; 1 Timothy 5:8).

The precious life of a woman should be lived in fearless freedom, so that she may become who God created her to be. Woman is a man's spiritual equal, his helper and earthly companion (Genesis 2:18; Galatians 3:28). In Christ, there are simply no women who hold a secondhand citizenship. The God Most High, El Elyon, the God of the Bible, of Abraham, Isaac and Jacob sent His Son Jesus to earth to die for our sins. Jesus is the only way to heaven; there is no other route. No manmade traditions or customs can attain a sinful woman's entrance to those heavenly heights (John 14:6).

Jesus, being perfect, sinless, fully God and fully Man, died for our sins on the cross and made us right in the eyes of a Holy God (1 Peter 1:18, 19; Hebrews 10:10, 28). The Scripture of John 3:16 says: *For God so loved the world that He gave His only begotten Son, that whoever believes in Him should not perish but have everlasting life.* It is a call to repent of our own sins and to accept Him as Savior. Salvation is an eternal reward to any woman, from any nation, who has the courage to accept Jesus Christ by faith.

The story of *Jesus of Nazareth*—the movie I watched long ago, when I sat sobbing alone, had caused me to question, *"Is there really a Man like this?"* Perhaps, after reading my story, you have been moved to silent tears. Do you relate to my story because of your own wounded life? Are you now questioning the reality of a *Man like this?* I tell you with my whole heart, Jesus is that Man! His one passion is for you to know Him personally as your own personal Savior, Healer and Deliverer.

You may be ready to put this book down and go on with an ordinary mundane life, but I hope not. Through opening the door to my personal life story, my desire for you is that the door to your own heart would be open to receive all that Christ has for you.

Satan wants you to keep the door of your heart locked. Jesus is the key to open it. He says: *Behold, I stand at the door and knock. If anyone hears My voice and opens the door, I will come into him and dine with him, and he with Me* (Revelation 3:20). He also declared: . . . *I am the First and the Last. I am He who lives, and was dead, and behold, I am alive forevermore . . . And I have the keys of Hades and of Death* (Revelations 1:17-18).

Believe me, this is a door you want to open, where you ask Jesus to come into your heart, as you accept the reality of His existence as the Son of God. As you do, a door of freedom opens; you are freed from sin and its penalty—death. Your own past, the sinful slate of your life is wiped clean, and you can enter a brand new life.

One of the Holy Spirit's symbols is that of wind, and it reminds me of the gentle breeze that blew against my face and made me feel alive on the day of my escape from my father. The Holy Spirit gives a regenerative, transforming life to those who are spiritually dead.

Jesus is gentle, a genuine Gentleman, and He will not force you to come to Him—to accept Him as Savior. But if He has drawn you to Himself, do not turn the other way. He can heal you of your past hurts, forgive you of your own sins and help you to forgive others. I pray you come to know this Man's love—God's love; for He is both fully human and fully divine.

If you desire to know Christ and experience His love, along with all I have described, please repeat this simple prayer and mean it with all your heart, by faith . . .

Dear Jesus,

You have known me before I was born and watched me grow as a child until now. You know all the hurts and sufferings I have been through. I understand that as an innocent Man, You willingly died for my sins on the cross. Thank You for loving me this way. I want to accept You as my Lord and Savior. Please forgive me of my own sins and fill my empty, broken heart with Your Holy Spirit. Heal any past wounds I have received in my life and help me to forgive others. In Jesus name I pray . . . Amen.

How wonderful! If you have said this simple prayer, you can rejoice and sing with me:

> Jesus paid it all,
> All to Him I owe;
> Sin had left a crimson stain,
> He washed it white as snow.

Written by Elvina Hall

A Figure of a Father

I would like to honor a man who became a figure of a father and the Christian patriarch of my growing family. My father-in-law, Alfred, was to me a gentle giant, fondly known as *Dad.*

His was the first welcome—the first embrace into his country, then his humble home, his heart and most importantly, his newly found Christian faith. Alfred showed genuine, loving care to this young English girl, now in America away from family and friends. He became a father to me—a reflection of my heavenly Father above—strong and protective, ever filled with unconditional love.

Although somewhat outwardly gruff, inwardly Alfred was a man who was tender and soft. His arms were strong and he would often hold me in times of great difficulty. His words were kind, and he often encouraged my weary soul, as I started a new beginning—a new life . . .

Sovereignly Designed

Ours was not a chance meeting;
It was by God's sovereign design
To remain a part of my history,
A father who was mine.

Our somber goodbye was
not to be a dismal ending,
As I kissed his bruised and aged brow.
To his daughter he whispered gently,
"Sweetheart,"
As he fell peacefully asleep for now.

There will be yet another
new bright beginning,
In a place where God's glory dwells.
Two souls will be reunited
in a hope that is never ending
And a love that never fails.

~Claire Wren~
In Loving Memory of Alfred Engeron

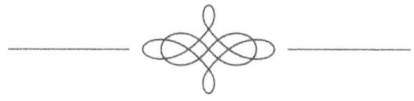

Chapter Six

BIBLICAL WISDOM CONCERNING SEXUAL ABUSE

One out of every six women will become a victim of rape or attempted rape at some time in their lives. RAINN, which stands for "Rape, Abuse & Incest National Network," is one of the nation's largest anti-sexual violence organizations. They gave these disturbing statements in the year of 2017.

Sexual Assault Statistics:

- Every 98 seconds, an American is sexually assaulted.

- Every 8 minutes, that victim is a child.

- One out of every 6 American women has been the victim of an attempted or complete rape in her lifetime.

- On average, there are 321,500 victims (age 12 or older) of rape and sexual assault each year in the United States.

- Ages 12-34 are the highest risk years for rape and sexual assault.

- 33% of women who are raped contemplate suicide.

- 13% of women attempt suicide.

- Out of the yearly 63,000 sexual abuse cases substantiated 80% of perpetrators were a parent.

- 93% of the recorded assaults are committed by someone the victim knows.

- Out of every 1000 rapes 994 perpetrators will walk free. The vast majority of perpetrators will not go to jail or prison.

- Sexual violence crimes not reported to police from 2005-2010, the victim gave the following reasons for not reporting:

  –20% feared retaliation

  –13% believed the police would not do anything to help

  –13% believed it was a personal matter

  –8% reported to a different official

  –8% believed it was not important enough to report

  –7% did not want to get the perpetrator in trouble

  –2% believed the police could not do anything to help

  –30% gave another reason, or did not cite one reason

Those unreported assaults can only mean that many violated women and young girls fearfully choose to hide what has happened to them. Unbeknownst to others their secret hurts are tucked away—a burdensome agony to carry.

Some victims even question and wonder if somehow it was their fault, and they take the blame upon themselves. Grief stricken, they find a place to shed their tears in private solitude.

So what happens to women and young girls who have been sexually violated? At worst, many end up in mental institutions, unable to cope with life. The crimes committed against them have pushed them mentally and emotionally over the edge. They may often stare blankly, too troubled to speak. In a sense, they simply stop living.

Within the victim's mind continue the dramatic scenes of their violation which constantly rewinds and replays like an endless videotape. Sleep offers little peace, as they suffer horrible nightmares that remind them of their sexual assault. These torturous dreams, often so real, keep fresh the pictures of what happened within their scarred and broken minds.

Suicide is contemplated as a way of escape from their mind and memories; it can become an alternative option—another way out instead of facing family, police or the fear of going to court.

For many younger victims, the terrifying reality of being taken away, to be placed in a foster home, is too great. Others do not want to cause drama, and cannot deal with other people's reactions. Instead, a victim may wrongly think the best way is just to die, so the secret would die with them.

Others have strong emotions that can result from the trauma—feelings of worthlessness, humiliation, disgrace, shame, guilt and regret. Most have a sense of being ruined, dirty, used and unclean. Depression, anxiety and deeply rooted fears often control their lives, fearful that an assault might happen again.

I have known girls who deliberately gain weight and wear oversized clothing, just so men will not notice them, whereas some are down-right angry, outraged over the crime, and become fierce haters of men.

Doctors and psychiatrists can listen and give therapeutic counsel to victims of sexual abuse. Medical professionals also use various prescription drugs to treat them. I am sure they hope to give them some temporal peace and relief to ease their minds and emotions from the horrendous, vivid memories that still torment them. But for many women, their violated lives will never be the same again.

Support groups offer sexually abused women and their families supportive counseling. Those severely distressed can draw comfort from each other's experiences and relate how they came to cope with the trauma. Many say they are empowered by these supportive sessions and victoriously call themselves survivors, while other women, perhaps unable to cope, choose to never talk or think about their experiences.

In denial, they move on in life shielded with a protective wall built around that secret part of their lives. The wall is impenetrable, making them invulnerable, so they can safely pretend the sexual abuse or violation never happened.

By no means am I a professional counselor, but I am a woman who knows God and has studied His Word, His amazing character, and divine attributes for over thirty-seven years. I can only give to others what I have received, and as you have read my testimony, I really believe it is Christ who found me! He is the One who brought healing and forgiveness into my life. So, I can take no credit, except to say, any wisdom imparted from my life is simply this— God working in a forgiven sinner's heart.

Therefore, I have a Christian responsibility to point others to Christ, who is all Wisdom. To direct others to myself would be extremely foolish; only God can bear such heavy burdens and free us from pain. Each situation is uniquely different, and God, who is omniscient, perfectly knows them all. I pray that He will be the One to give you the wisdom you need.

There will be those of you who will express a deep gratitude for my open transparency in sharing my personal testimony—thankful for what you may have gleaned and found helpful. On the other hand, I am aware that there may be those who will oppose the writing of such a story and disagree with the answers I have written.

But the Book I have not penned is the authoritative pages of the Bible. I believe there is unlimited wisdom found in its passages that can bring divine support, healing and comfort for all those who have been victims of sexual abuse (James 1:5).

As uncomfortable a subject as sexual abuse may be, I have found that many women have common questions. Answers to these questions can be talked about in the seemingly private pages of my book. I can honestly say I wish I didn't have any knowledge or experience with the subject of sexual abuse, but I do. Many women have spoken to me about their own stories, and I have counseled with girls as young as eight and women as old as sixty. Each life has benefited in some way. Most have been touched spiritually, whether finding salvation, healing or peace, which beforehand had eluded them.

Wise Words of Understanding

QUESTION: If there is a God of love, why did He allow this to happen to me?

Rest assured, there is a God of love (John 3:16; 1 John 4:8). God never intended for you to be harmed, and for this critical question, let me take some time in explanation. Each man and woman is created with a free will. At a certain age, comes the understanding of what is right and what is wrong. Man has a free will to choose his actions. If a choice is made to harm another, innocent people will suffer.

In the beginning, God's design was for mankind to live in total obedience to His Word. His will was for a loving, sexual relationship to be only between a husband and a wife (Genesis 2:18-25; 4:1). The Bible gives us clear understanding about sexual relationships. Any deviation from that original design brings confusion and sexual depravity.

But in Genesis, Chapter 3, man rebelled against God and disobeyed His Word, casting the whole human race into a fallen state of sin. From that point on, we read the graphic accounts of sexual degeneracy. The Bible doesn't hide the evil of man's sin, and the true stories of women who were violated are quite explicit.

In Chapter 6, we find women who were violated by demons. A quote from *The New Unger's Bible*

Dictionary explains further: *This utterly unnatural union violated God's created order of being and was such a shocking abnormality as to necessitate the world wide judgment of the flood.*

Yet, it didn't take long for sexual perversion to continue in the pages of the Bible. By Genesis, Chapter 19, in Sodom and Gomorrah, we find Lot's daughters under the threat of violation. Incest happened in Genesis 19:30-38, when Lot's daughters thought it was the end of their world and violated themselves. They lay sexually with their father, and they birthed the Moabite and Ammonite nations.

Then in Genesis 34:2, Dinah, the daughter of Jacob, was defiled—raped by Prince Shechem: *And when Shechem the son of Hamor the Hivite, prince of the country, saw her, he took her and lay with her, and violated her.*

In 2 Samuel Chapter 13, a lustful plot is unraveled. Tamar, attending to the needs of her supposedly sick, half-brother Amnon, is violated, raped and shamed.

Then in Judges 19:22-29, you will find a vicious story of gang rape and murder at Gibeah. It is one of the most brutal stories I have ever read. The debased men of the city *knew* her (sexually) and abused her all night until morning, and when the day began to break, they let her go. Reaching the steps of where she was staying, she died.

Even in biblical times, laws of justice within Israel were in place to protect virgins and maidens when any kind of violation occurred.

By Deuteronomy 22:25-29, those who violated others were subject to swift judgment.

QUESTION: Why would someone in my very own family hurt me this way?

The answer, quite simply, is sin. The root of my father's sin was discovered by my siblings. Pornography was hidden under the mattress of my parents' double bed. As a Christian adult, I began to understand that my father's sin of lust was fed by pornography. These debased magazines were a tool that stimulated my father's lust for sex—a craving that, no matter the cost, must be satisfied. Pornography helped turn my father into a pedophile. Pornography twisted a man who should have been a protective father towards his little daughters. Later in life, he should have been a decent, loving grandfather—instead, he became a child molester, and that is how he will always be remembered.

Wise Words about Forgiveness

QUESTION: Do I have to forgive the person who has hurt me?

The biblical answer is yes, but to many, this answer seems unjust and unfair. You may reason, *Why should any person who has been hurt be the one to forgive? It should be the one who hurt me who should be apologizing!*

I attended a seminar once, and the speaker had said, "You can choose to forgive or not to forgive." However, Jesus taught us unforgiveness is very harmful, because it has many bitter and eternal consequences (Matthew 6:12, 14-15). Despite the horrendous ordeal you may have been through as a victim of sexual abuse, the Bible teaches us to forgive those who have committed sinful offenses against us. This is something you cannot do on your own; it is only through the power of the Holy Spirit (Zechariah 4:6).

I had counseled a woman struggling with forgiveness due to sexual abuse, she just needed to grasp more on what forgiveness felt like. Is it a feeling, an action or just a decision? She had so much anger and rage over the injustice of it all, that she had continued to hold on to unforgiveness for years. She was as frank and honest as she could be. The woman voiced her fear of dying with the sin of unforgiveness in her heart. She greatly desired peace to replace her emotional ups and downs. Still being tormented by terrible nightmares, she finally reached out for help. It seemed so calloused just to give her a cliché answer, "Well, the Bible says you need to forgive, so just forgive and go forward."

After so much hurt, she deserved a well-thought-out answer. The Bible sheds so much light on the subject of forgiveness, both in the Old Testament and in the New Testament. In the Hebrew language, forgiveness of sin has always been based on sacrifice. Atonement[55] was made to pay for sin through the shedding of blood; an animal was killed (Leviticus 4), whereby the sinner was forgiven.

This picture is mirrored for us perfectly in the New Testament. In Ephesians 1:7, Jesus' blood is shed for our forgiveness: *In Him we have redemption through His blood, the forgiveness of sins, according to the riches of His grace.* Forgiveness for our sin did not cost us anything, but it cost Christ everything.

On Yom Kippur—the Jewish Day of Atonement, sins were transferred to a scapegoat. The animal was then released to wander in the wilderness (Leviticus 16), just as our sins are *sent away* as far as the east is from the west. In the Greek language, one of the New Testament words for forgiveness literally

---

[55] Atonement: the reconciliation of God and humankind through the sacrificial death of Jesus Christ. God restored the world to Himself, no longer counting men's sins against them but blotting them out (2 Corinthians 5:19-20).

means, *send away.* To receive such forgiveness, we must confess our sin and repent of it.

Understanding how forgiveness happens will lead you to act in obedience and, by faith in God's Word, forgive others (Matthew 6:14-15, Ephesians 4:32). His healing, through forgiveness, enables you to be free and move forward, unhindered by your past! Once free from your bitterness, anger and resentment, forgiveness becomes the medicine to heal your open wounds The Great Physician Jesus gives us the prescription of forgiveness—the only remedy to help heal deep wounds inflicted on us by others.

In our relationship with God, we can pour out all the emotions we have held onto—anger, bitterness and anguish—and cry out to Him in prayer. He listens. God patiently waits for you to release to Him the burden and hurt you have carried all these long years.

I can imagine Jesus endearingly pleading with us as we struggle, "Daughter, give that to Me; let Me take that for you. What you have gone through has been too burdensome for you to carry."Comfortingly, Jesus might say, "Daughter, simply yield it up to Me in complete surrender. Let Me have that and finally let go. Now you have given that area of your life to Me, lay it aside and let it alone." The truth of the matter is that the dreadful past has to be let go, so you can move freely forward (Philippians 3:13).

If these wounds are not taken care of, they will only fester, bleed and continue to weep like an inner poison, which will persist in causing you so much pain. Gaze at the cross, for here is our example in forgiving others. In Luke 23:34, Jesus hung in agonizing pain on the cross, pain that was inflicted on Him by sinners; yet He cried: *"Father, forgive them, for they do not know what they do!"*

QUESTION: Once I have forgiven the person who has sexually abused me, do I have to socialize or interact with them in any way?

I believe, through Christ, forgiveness can restore any relationship where sexual abuse has occurred. That miracle comes from the Lord. However, it is important to realize that, even though you can forgive someone, if there has been no real change or repentance, they are still capable of repeating the same, awful crimes. Understand, you can forgive your perpetrator but that doesn't mean you have to socialize with them. You must be careful not to get entrapped by them again.

This is especially applicable to a victim who is a child and has been abused by a family member. It could mean, for example, a grandfather not seeing his granddaughter again, and, although forgiven, that is something he would just have to live with. It is important for parents/guardians to understand that they need to protect a child from any further sexual abuse and not be overly concerned with the hurt feelings of the abuser.

For most victims, trust has to be rebuilt. It may take a long time before you begin to trust that person again. Then again, trust may never be restored. If you no longer feel safe or comfortable around that person, you should never feel forced to give them a hug or socialize with them. For your own peace of mind, you may need to stay completely away from the individual.

Wise Words about Reporting

QUESTION: If I am being molested or violated, how can I get help now?

If you are being sexually abused now, do not remain silent. The person violating you will have you trapped, while the abuse remains a secret, and the sexual abuse will continue. Do not allow them to commit these awful crimes against you. Remember, there are laws in place to protect you. Tell someone and break the silence now; do not wait until it happens again. I know this will take a lot of courage, but please speak to a trusted family member, a pastor or a teacher at school or college. If frightened, take a friend and go file a report at the police station.

Sexual abuse victims can shut down emotionally, but let me try to help you THINK! Here are some basic survival tactics that will help save you from further harm.

GET OUT!   SPEAK OUT!   STAY OUT!

You need to be informed about the well-known agencies ready and waiting to take seriously your call for help:

Report Abuse: 1-800-656 (Hope) or 1-800-656-4673
Website: info@rainn.org

If in immediate danger, call 911.

Wise Words about Life

QUESTION: When I feel like I want to commit suicide, what should I do?

Please get the help and support you need now! Contact someone you trust—a known pastor, family member, friend or anyone available you can turn to who can speak with you immediately. You may feel utterly hopeless and that life is not worth living, but your life has great worth. It is vitally important that you do not let your feelings and overwhelming emotions lead you at this critical time. Get hold of those desperate thoughts! It is senseless to throw away the precious gift of your life when there is help to relieve the circumstances that have driven you to these extremes. Remember, you are not alone; help is available. When you feel like you cannot go on, call:

US Suicide Hot Line: 1-800-273-8255

From a Christian perspective, Satan is a thief. He wants to steal, kill and destroy, but Jesus came so that you may have an abundant life (John 10:10). Your eyes may be fixed on the trauma you are experiencing, but don't be robbed of the life Christ intends to give you. Remember, your life has so much worth that Christ gave His life for yours!

QUESTION: I am afraid and worried about what happens in my family if I speak up. What if everybody gets angry towards me?

Some family members may get angry, but do not let fear stop you from speaking up. You have been injured and need your family's support. It is never pleasant to expose sexual abuse, but you must, if you want the abuse to stop. If there is no one in your family to help you, then surround yourself with people outside your family circle who are willing to love and support you through this difficult time. You may need to have a neutral place to stay until emotions calm down.

Along with yourself, any immediate and surrounding family members will also share with you in the shame, anger and a whole host of emotional ups and downs. Once the crime is exposed, the news hits like an atomic bomb, and the blast causes a terrible ripple effect throughout the entire family. The emotions and reactions can be extreme, especially if the perpetrator was someone trusted and close within your family, such as a father, grandfather or uncle.

It has been known for some family members to place blame for the sexual abuse on the victim. They may grapple in disbelief and denial since the truth is hard to swallow. As abusers are often very good at manipulating another person's emotions, some family members may have sympathy for the molester. No matter what happens, you are not at fault! Let the Lord deal with the hearts of others, even those who may turn against you. Remember, this is not just about you because there might be someone else in your family who is being sexually abused, as well. You may not be the only person abused, or who will be abused in the future, if you do not break the silence and speak up.

QUESTION: Is it my fault that the person who hurt me went to jail?

No! The Bible teaches the truth of sowing and reaping (Galatians 6:7-9). In other words, a person can be forgiven for what they have done, but their actions will still have consequences. For the perpetrator, that might mean jail time. Even if they are sorry for what they have done, the law was broken, and there will be penalties. In no way is that your fault, and no condemnation should ever be thrust upon you. Stand on Romans 8:1: *There is therefore now no condemnation to those who are in Christ Jesus, who do not walk according to the flesh, but according to the Spirit.*

Remember, you should never be forced to bear the guilt of someone else's sin or the results of their sin, including being sent to jail because of their own crimes committed against you.

Wise Words about Boundaries

QUESTION: How can I protect myself from being violated again?

It may be useful to use these three R's:

RECOGNIZE, RESIST, RUN

Recognize: Set healthy boundaries regarding your own personal space or inappropriate remarks directed towards you. Be very aware of your surroundings, and discern early signs of danger. Are there sexual comments being made towards you? Was there an inappropriate touch? Has any behavior made you feel uncomfortable? Any one of these actions can be a *Red Flag*, which lets you know something is not quite right.

Resist: When somebody crosses your boundaries, be firm and strong in your responses. You do not have to be polite. Learn how to fight back; you can say, for example, "I do not appreciate your comment; it was inappropriate. It stops now, or I will report what you have said." In the same way, strongly put a stop to any advances that have crossed your set boundaries. Remove yourself quickly from the location and, like the plague, avoid the person. For accountability, don't be afraid to let someone else know what happened.

Run: Stay within a group of people. Never be coaxed to be alone with someone you do not know well. Even if it is someone you know, and you just don't feel right, find a way of escape and get out! Run! Educate yourself and take advantage of the many websites on how not to become a victim of sexual assault. It may even be beneficial to take a self-defense course.

QUESTION: Why do I find it so hard to say no to sexual advances?

Once violated, especially if you were a child, you may remain vulnerable to other violators. Once you have been a victim of sexual abuse, you have been trained to be silent and almost sweetly submissive to sexual advances. You have learned to yield and give in to an abuser's sexual requests. Maybe you even protect the person, because you don't want them to get into trouble.

As a past victim, you have become easy to intimidate and frighten into submission. Fear again comes into play, and you yield in order to avoid them getting angry when you try to say no. The Bible teaches: *The fear of man brings a snare, but whoever trusts in the LORD shall be safe* (Proverbs 29:25). Stand your ground! It is acceptable to speak firmly, even if it seems rude. Let them know you are not an easy prey or target!

After being sexually abused, some girls may become very promiscuous. The Bible, in the book of Song of Solomon 2:7, tells a young woman, *Do not stir up nor awaken love until it pleases.* The right time is intended for marriage. During sexual abuse, some girls found the abuse was pleasurable, and those passions were awakened. Ask the Lord for the strength and self-control in not yielding to those awakened passions (Song of Solomon 8:4, Romans 6).

Wise Words about Restoration

QUESTION: I feel dirty and ruined. Is anybody going to want me?

Most victims of sexual violation feel this way, even though it wasn't their fault. God's Word washes you and makes you clean. It is like taking a bath, and the filthiness of what took place is washed away, making you feel brand new (2 Corinthians 5:17, Ephesians 5:26). Even our own sinful state is forgiven once we have repented—we become white as snow! (Isaiah 1:18)

God always reassures us of His divine love. In Song of Solomon, a young Shulamite girl felt unattractive and unworthy to be looked upon by the King whose eyes beheld her. Yet, his loving gaze was not dissuaded. He saw her beauty and addressed her as, *"O fairest among women"* (Song of Solomon 1:8).

Do you know you have worth in the eyes of God who made heaven and earth? He sees you as pure and innocent, and He loves you with an everlasting love (Jeremiah 31:3). When the time comes, He can bring into your life the person who loves you as Christ does, no matter what has happened in the past.

QUESTION: If I was molested by a person of my own sex does that mean I am a lesbian or a homosexual?

No! Often young girls who have been molested question their own sexuality, especially if the molestation was by a woman. I have known girls to think, *Is there something wrong with me for a woman to have molested me? So, perhaps I am a lesbian.* This is also true of boys who have been molested by men. They too, question their sexual identity, thinking they are homosexuals.

However, biblically this is not true! There is much sexual confusion in our society today. God is not the author of confusion, and as Creator, by His design, marriage is intended to be the unification of one man and one woman. Anything outside of that created order and design is unnatural (1 Corinthians 14:33).

I have understood that being sexually abused by a man can steer women away from trusting men altogether. Men who have violated women have caused them such pain that, instead of seeking a healthy relationship with a man, they are easily seduced into lesbian relationships. Emotions and society aside, what does the Bible teach? Read Romans 1, in its entirety, and let the truth set you free!

QUESTION: I suffer from terrible nightmares that remind me of the sexual abuse. What can help?

Prayer and more prayer . . . when you have suffered such trauma in your life, often nightmares will come. Post-traumatic stress disorder is a real psychological condition, caused from the disturbing situations of violent abuse. Even those who have gone to war and experienced terrifying atrocities suffer from the disorder. But through prayer and God's Word, you can overcome. Perhaps you can call a trusted friend to pray with you and help you through these tough times—someone who will have Christ's compassion, and just listen, understand and pray. Know that dreams, no matter how disturbing, are just dreams . . . and as time goes by and the Lord heals you, they will become but mere shadows of the fading past.

Wise Words about Going Forward

QUESTION: How can I ever go forward? Why do some people in my life not understand why it is so difficult for me?

Some people may say to a person who has gone through sexual abuse, "Well, can't you just get over it now and move forward?" Some people can be ignorantly heartless; they unfortunately lack the understanding of sexual abuse and how it has impacted a person's life. Everyone has their own breaking point.

Nobody should ever belittle what has happened to you, whether it seems minor or major to them. You, as well as all other victims, need compassion. Many girls have been truly broken and will need support and love from loyal friends and family for a long time.

Jesus had unlimited compassion for people around Him who were hurt and in need of His healing touch (Matthew 9:35-36). It is through Christ, I believe, that you can move forward. In pointing girls to Christ, I have always tried to develop their relationship with Him by teaching studies that relate to His character. Some girls have had a difficult time verbally expressing the horrible details of their abuse. These young women find relief in writing them down, and often they are able to communicate on paper their immense rage over what has happened to them.

There is life after sexual abuse. I know this from experience. Always go forward one step at a time, and do not look back. Do not let what has happened in the past hinder you from going forward. It is never good to live in the past or to keep reliving the past by speaking about the abuse over and over again. Do not remain the frightened victim from the past. Philippians 3:13-14 tells us . . . *but one thing I do, forgetting those things which are behind and reaching forward to those things which are ahead, I press toward the goal for the prize of the upward call of God in Christ Jesus.*

You can enjoy living a victorious, new future in Christ. His Word tells us: *For I know the thoughts that I think toward you, says the LORD, thoughts of peace and not of evil, to give you a future and a hope* (Jeremiah 29:11).

QUESTION: Are there any drawbacks from receiving secular counseling?

The intent of this book is to convey a spiritual message. It has not been written with any secular counsel or in any way to challenge other methods that offer help to sexually abused women. I know women who have gone to secular counseling, benefitted greatly from their support, and are grateful for what they have received.

Someone close to me gained tremendous support from a woman who was a mental health professional.

She met with her once a week and continued to talk with her for over ten years.

However, I have observed some drawbacks from women who have received secular counseling, and it is good to be aware of those issues if you choose this route:

Man's Wisdom: In secular counseling, there is no Christ-centered counsel, and it is my belief that, from a spiritual standing, there is much wisdom lost. A woman is not ministered to in the depths of her soul. Her spirit is often left broken when sexually abused. You may ask, "Is there such a thing as a broken spirit?" King David described himself as having a broken spirit, as he repented before the Lord for his adultery. Psalm 51:17 says: *The sacrifices of God are a broken spirit, a broken and a contrite heart—These, O God, You will not despise.* Only God can heal the broken spirited and heal a broken heart.

Dependency: A woman can rely or depend on the counselor or support group during their whole life time. The sexual abuse becomes central to their life and is spoken about over and over again. These types of sessions seem to hinder a woman from moving forward. Frankly, the only time I talk openly about sexual abuse is to help another person. Other than that, it is not on my mind at all. I am too busy enjoying the life the Lord has blessed me with!

<u>Victim Mentality</u>: Talking about your abuse all the time can lead to what secular counselors would call a "victim mentality." Having a victim mentality is a very depressing and hopeless state of mind. You feel trapped as if what has happened to you now determines your failed future. You may think, *I am this way now, and there is no hope. I cannot go forward; I can never let go of what happened to me and leave it all behind. It is on the forefront of my mind every day.* So now the way you act and behave is all based on your abusive past. It will never change or improve. You feel your life is in ruins, and it was entirely the abuser's fault.

There is nothing like rebuilding your life and getting to know who you are in Christ (1 Peter 2:9). Your value and your worth come from Him (Matthew 10:29-31). Imagine a broken wall that needs to be rebuilt—let God rebuild your life one brick at a time! (Song of Solomon 8:9)

<u>Self-Empowerment</u>: This type of teaching rebuilds a person's self-esteem by purely exalting self. It is the idea that now you have broken away from your abuser, you have regained the power and control they once had over you. Now you have a self-determined life. It is the mind-set that says, "I am in control, independent and have created my own safe haven!" You hold the power over your own life and destiny. You are no longer a victim, and you have the power to forgive or not to forgive your abuser. You look for other ways to make yourself feel more empowered.

You believe you can do it all on your own and you seek to empower other survivors of sexual abuse.

I believe this develops an unattractive and sinful pride in people's lives. Just go back over the above paragraph and circle the word "you." Where is God in this picture? The truth is, when He comes into your life, He gives you the power, through the Holy Spirit, to live the Christian life (Acts 1:8). In fact, the Bible says that without God, we can do nothing (John 15:5). He gives you the strength to go forward; He provides your emotional and spiritual needs; He helps you to grow as a person. God empowers you to share what He has done for you with other hurting women. In our lives, we should give Him all the thanks, glory and honor. Think on this hymn, "To God be the Glory" by Fanny Jane Crosby:

> To God be the glory, great things He has done,
> So loved He the world that He gave us His Son,
> Who yielded His life, an atonement for sin,
> And opened the life-gate that all may go in.

> Praise the Lord, praise the Lord,
> Let the earth hear His voice;
> Praise the Lord, praise the Lord,
> Let the people rejoice;

> Oh, come to the Father,
> through Jesus the Son,
> And give Him the Glory;
> great things He hath done.

So you see, it is quite the opposite of this self–empowerment mentality and philosophy.

QUESTION: Will I ever be *normal* or will I need counseling for the rest of my life?

Good question! Well, what is constituted as normal? Are any of us normal? It brings a smile to my face really, because we all have problems, hang- ups, insecurities and the list goes on. For life and its many problems, I would once again direct you to Christ—our Wonderful Counselor who promises to never leave you and is always there to listen. There is no one who knows you more than the Creator of heaven and earth. He knows each tear; He knows how many hairs are on your head, your fears and anxieties. He is the great I AM!! Not only will He counsel us about our past, but our present and future. We are in good hands! I cannot and will not point you to anyone else except Jesus Christ our *Wonderful, Counselor* and *Prince of Peace* (Isaiah 9:6).

Wise Words of Warning

QUESTION: I feel so angry at the injustice of being sexually abused, and I want to cause the person who violated me harm. Isn't that justifiable, seeing what harm they have done to me?

It is good to understand that no matter how angry you may become, you should not take matters into your own hands. In the book of James, written by James, the half-brother to Jesus, he instructs the beloved believers in Christ that *the wrath* [anger] *of man does not produce the righteousness of God* (James 1:20). In other words, your anger and desire for retaliation, no matter how justifiable you think they are, do not match up with God's equity—His justice or His holy character.

If the person who violated you never truly repents from their actions and never receives forgiveness for their sins through Jesus Christ, they will stand before God on the Day of Judgment and He will hold them accountable. They will face a final judgment, without mercy, and experience eternal torment in the depths of hell (Matthew 25:46, 1 Thessalonians 1:6-9, Hebrews 9:27).

To those who are responsible for violating young, innocent victims, the Bible issues a stiff warning. Matthew 18:6-7, 10 tells us, It is better that a millstone was hung around your neck and thrown into the depths of the sea than to harm one of these little ones . . . Take heed that you do not despise one of these little ones, for I say to you that in heaven their angels always see the face of My Father who is in heaven.

Imagine, their angels see the face of God. I would seriously think twice about hurting a child or any innocent person, because God will repay that wickedness.

QUESTION: How can God make good come out of something so terrible?

In my teenage years, my life could have tragically ended. To look back now and see the wonderful plan of God unfolding over these years has been truly amazing! To think of the incredible blessings that would have been stolen from me if my life had been cut short!

What is more exciting is that God is not finished yet, and there are more blessings yet to come! My life has become so rich! I have four children I never thought I would have and three, boisterous, joy-of-my-heart grandchildren. The Lord has used my life to identify and help girls and women who have suffered sexual abuse.

The Bible teaches that God has a plan and purpose for each of us: *"For I know the thoughts that I think towards you, says the Lord, thoughts of peace and not of evil, to give you a future and a hope* (Jeremiah 29:11). Although bad circumstances happen in our lives, God has a way of making things work out for good in the end as Romans 8:28 tells us: *And we know that all things work together for good to those who love God, to those who are the called according to His purpose* (Romans 8:28).

I would like you to think about this question: What do you think Christ has in store for your own life? Read, this Scripture and be encouraged!

But as it is written:
"Eye has not seen, nor ear heard,
Nor have entered into the heart of man
The things which God has prepared
for those who love Him."

1 CORINTHIANS 2:9

References:

Cambridge Advanced Learners Dictionary and Thesaurus

Cambridge Academic Content Dictionary

Cambridge University Press, Wikipedia, Collins English Dictionary

The Phrase Finder